Avenues
Practice Book

HAMPTON-BROWN

Contents

Unit 4 | Watery World

Unit 5 | Cultural Ties

Unit 6 | This State of Mine

Unit 7 | What's It Worth?

Unit 8 | Rocky Tales

Name _____ Date _____

Vocabulary: Key Words

Clothes to Share

Key Words
brand-new
hand-me-down
mind
notice
outgrown
proudly
refuse
style

  Read each sentence.

Circle the word that completes each sentence correctly. Then write the sentence.

1. I wear my sister's __(hand-me-down)/ notice__ dresses.

   I wear my sister's hand-me-down dresses.

2. I don't care if they are not __brand-new / proudly__.

   _____

3. I never __outgrown / refuse__ to wear the clothes she gives me.

   _____

4. People always __brand-new / notice__ my sister's clothes.

   _____

5. She has such great __style / hand-me-down__!

   _____

6. When she has __outgrown / notice__ the clothes, I get the style!

   _____

7. I also don't __mind / style__ that the clothes are free.

   _____

8. I __proudly / style__ wear everything she gives me.

   _____

Name _____ Date _____

Buy Those Shoes!

 Read each sentence type.

 **Rewrite each sentence.
Use correct capitalization
and end punctuation.**

> **Sentence Types**
>
> A **statement** tells something. It begins with a capital letter and ends with a period.
>
> An **exclamation** shows strong feeling. It begins with a capital letter and ends with an exclamation mark.
>
> A **command** tells someone to do something. It begins with a capital letter and ends with a period or an exclamation mark.

1. ⬚ Statement ⬚ these are my new shoes

These are my new shoes.

2. ⬚ Command ⬚ tell me if you like them

_____

3. ⬚ Exclamation ⬚ these shoes are so comfortable

_____

4. ⬚ Command ⬚ buy a pair for me

_____

5. ⬚ Statement ⬚ we will go to the store tomorrow

_____

6. ⬚ Command ⬚ go get them now

_____

7. ⬚ Statement ⬚ I will come with you

_____

8. ⬚ Exclamation ⬚ they look great on you

_____

© Hampton-Brown

Name _____ Date _____

This Sentence Is Complete!

 Look at each group of words below.

Write COMPLETE beside each complete sentence. Write INCOMPLETE beside each group of words that is not a complete sentence.

Check your work with a partner.

Complete Sentences

- A sentence is a complete thought. It has a **subject** and a **predicate**.
- The **subject** tells whom or what the sentence is about.
- The **predicate** tells what the subject is, does, or has.

_____Incomplete_____ **1.** This black shoe.

_____ **2.** Rigo wears hand-me-down clothes.

_____ **3.** Bought a pair of shoes.

_____ **4.** Marched down the street.

_____ **5.** These are beautiful shoes.

 Look at the chart.

Write a subject or predicate to complete each sentence.

Choose from the chart or use your own.

Subjects	Predicates
My jacket	plays football
My mom	bought a jacket
My dad	was expensive
Her white dress	looks cute

6. This new hat _____.

7. _____ buys all my clothes.

8. My older brother _____.

9. _____ is too small.

© Hampton-Brown

Grammar: Complete Sentences

What's It All About?

 Read each sentence.

 Write STATEMENT or COMMAND below each sentence.

Then write the subject.

> ### The Subject
> The subject tells whom or what the sentence is about.
>
> In a **command**, the subject is not named, but it is always "you."

1. Put on your shoes.

_Command: You_____

2. These old shoes are too tight.

_____

3. My cousin Perry has new shoes.

_____

4. Denise and Marie need new shoes.

_____

5. We will get some at the shoe store.

_____

6. Show me the fancy sneakers.

_____

7. These loafers are my favorite.

_____

8. Try them on now!

_____

9. They look very nice.

_____

10. Aunt Rosa will buy them for you.

_____

MORE Complete Sentences

👥 Work with a partner. ✏️ Write a sentence together. You start the sentence with a subject. Your partner completes the sentence with a predicate.

Graphic Organizer: Character Chart

If the Shoe Fits

📖 Review "If the Shoe Fits."

✏️ Complete the character chart for Rigo.

Events →	Rigo's Feelings →	Rigo's Actions
Rigo gets new shoes for his birthday.	Rigo feels happy and proud.	Rigo puts nickels in his shoes and wears them proudly.
Angel tells Rigo that his shoes are stupid.		
Rigo gets an invitation to a party.		
Rigo sees that his uncle's clothes are old.		

© Hampton-Brown

Vocabulary Strategy

Context Clues

Read the passage below. Think about how to use context clues.

A Beautiful Dress

1   It was finally the end of the school year. Mina was going to the big dance.

2   She said to her mom, "I need a new dress for the prom. I have nothing to wear!"

3   Her mother said, "You have a nice green dress."

4   Mina answered, "No, that's a *short* dress! I want a long, fancy dress. Can you buy me a gown to wear?"

5   Mina's mother said, "Let's look in my closet. I may have a gown you can wear." Mina cried, "Oh no! I can't wear *your* gown to the dance! I want a new dress in the latest style."

6   "Well, let's look," said her mother. "I think I have a dress you might like." Mina's mother pulled a long dress from her closet. Mina looked at the gown and smiled. The dress was dark blue with shiny beads around the top. It was such a great dress!

7   Mina cried, "This is a wonderful dress! Where did you buy this marvelous dress?"

8   "You know I love to sew, Mina," said her mother. "I worked on this dress for months. I wanted to make your gown for the prom."

9   Mina threw her arms around her mother. "Thank you for such a beautiful dress!" she said.

Now take the test on page 11.

Test Strategy

Try to answer the question without reading the answer choices. Then compare your answer to the choices.

Read each item. Choose the best answer.

1   Read paragraphs 1 and 2 on page 10.

What does the word <u>prom</u> mean?

- a big room
- a boy who dances
- a fancy car used to go to a dance
- a special dance at the end of the school year

2   Read paragraph 4 on page 10.

What does the word <u>gown</u> mean?

- a big hat
- a green dress
- a long, fancy dress
- a pair of shoes

3   Read paragraphs 6 and 7 on page 10.

Which words help you know what <u>marvelous</u> means?

- was; such
- great; wonderful
- Mina cried
- this; dress

Understand and Use Idioms

 Read each sentence.

Circle the correct meaning for the idiom.

1. My brother was **playing with fire**. He took my shirt without asking me first.

   - He did something dangerous.

   - He played with matches.

   - He danced around a campfire.

2. I told him I was going to **spill the beans** about what he did.

   - I was going to pour beans onto a table.

   - I was going to tell the secret.

   - I was going to plant beans in the garden.

3. He was really **down in the dumps** when I said that.

   - He was at the town dump.

   - He fell on the ground.

   - He was very sad.

4. I told him not to worry because I was just **pulling his leg**.

   - I was holding his foot and pulling hard.

   - I wanted him to go for a walk with me.

   - I was just teasing him.

Name _____ Date _____

Let's Communicate!

Key Words
communicate
experience
imagination
publish
remind
reply

 Read the paragraph.

✏ **Write the correct Key Word to complete each sentence.**

I want to write about a fun _____
1.

I had at the park last summer. I love to write. It helps to

_____ me of things I have done. It feels good to
2.

_____ all my thoughts and feelings to other people.
3.

I can use the ideas in my head, my _____,
4.

to make up great stories! It's fun to write letters to friends,

too! If you write me a letter, I will _____
5.

right away. Someday I want to

_____ a book
6.

of short stories.

MORE Key Words Practice

👥 Ask a partner to use one Key Word in a sentence. Then
your partner can choose a Key Word for you to use.

Name _____ Date _____

Ask and Answer Questions

 Read the question words.

 Ask questions about "In Gary Soto's Shoes." Answer your partner's questions.

✏ **Write the questions and answers.**

Capitals and End Marks

- Start all questions and answers with a capital letter.
- End all questions with a question mark.
- End all answers with a period or an exclamation mark.

> **Question:** Does Gary Soto like to write?
> **Answer:** Yes, he loves to write!

Is	Are

1. Question: _____

Answer: _____

Do	Does

2. Question: _____

Answer: _____

Who	What	When	Where

3. Question: _____

Answer: _____

4. Question: _____

Answer: _____

Name _____ Date _____

Do You Communicate?

🖉 Write a question on each question line. Start each question with *Do* or *Does*.

🏃🏃 Trade papers with a partner.

🖉 Answer your partner's questions.

Questions with *Do* and *Does*

Some questions ask for a **yes** or **no** answer. You can use **do** and **does** to ask **yes / no** questions.

• When the answer is **yes**, say **do** or **does**.

• When the answer is **no**, say **don't** or **doesn't**.

1. Question: **Do** you like to use e-mail? _____

   Answer: Yes, I do. _____

2. Question: **Does** _____

   Answer: _____

3. Question: **Do** _____

   Answer: _____

4. Question: **Does** _____

   Answer: _____

5. Question: **Do** _____

   Answer: _____

6. Question: **Does** _____

   Answer: _____

Graphic Organizer: Turning-Point Map

In Gary Soto's Shoes

 Review "In Gary Soto's Shoes."

✏ Complete the turning-point map.

As a Child

1. Gary's father died.

2. He played baseball with his brother and looked for gardening jobs.

3.

4.

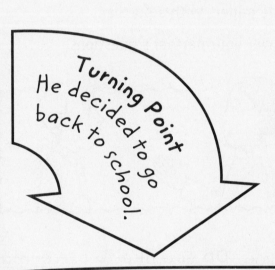

Turning Point He decided to go back to school.

As a Young Adult

1.

2.

3.

As an Adult

1.

2.

3.

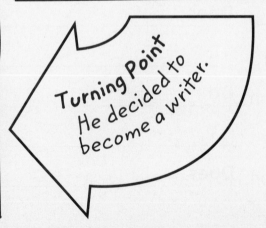

Turning Point He decided to become a writer.

© Hampton-Brown

Name _____ Date _____

Scrambled Sentences

 Look at each group of words.

Put the words in the correct order to make a sentence.

🖉 Write the sentence on the line.

1. you   Do   clothes?   new   have

Do you have new clothes?

2. wear   I   clothes.   hand-me-down

_____

3. brother   shirt.   me   gave   My   his

_____

4. blue   Is   the   or   shirt   red?

_____

5. is   It   blue.   dark

_____

6. want   I   too.   clothes,   hand-me-down

_____

MORE Sentences

🖉 Write a new sentence. Copy each word on a different card.

👥 Ask a classmate to put the words in the correct order.

Comprehension Skill

Facts and Opinions

 Read the e-mail.

Use one color to highlight each fact. Use another color to highlight each opinion.

Facts and Opinions

- A **fact** is a statement that you can check. Facts often include names, numbers, dates, or places.

- An **opinion** tells what someone thinks or feels. Opinions often use words like "I like" or "I believe."

FROM: Ronnie

TO: Gary Soto

SUBJECT: Uncles

Dear Mr. Soto,

I love your story "If the Shoe Fits." In my opinion, the best part is when Rigo gives Uncle Celso his shoes. I really like Uncle Celso. I have an uncle, too. My uncle is not a waiter. He is a fireman. His name is Robert. I think he is the greatest uncle in the world.

Your friend,

Ronnie

MORE Facts and Opinions

 Write two sentences about a book or story you have read. Make one sentence a fact. Make the other sentence an opinion.

Name _____ Date _____

Vocabulary: Key Words

A Feast for All

 Read each sentence.

Rewrite each sentence. Replace each word or phrase in dark print with a Key Word.

Key Words
agreed
chief
pole
push up
signal
tribe
village

1. Many people live in the **small group of houses**.

Many people live in the village.

2. The **leader** calls his people for a special meeting.

_____

3. His **people, who share the same ancestors,** will prepare a feast.

_____

4. Everyone **had the same idea**. The tribe must work together!

_____

5. The food will hang from a **long piece of wood**.

_____

6. The people work together to **lift** the pole.

_____

7. The people will use a **word to let everyone know** when the feast is ready.

_____

Grammar: Possessive Nouns

The Tribe's Big Problem

 Read the page in "Pushing Up the Sky."

Then answer the question on this page. Write a complete sentence. Be sure to add *'s* for each possessive noun.

> **Possessive Nouns**
>
> A **possessive noun** ends in **'s**. It tells who or what belongs to someone.
>
> Tom**'s** mother is the chief**'s** daughter.

page 80   **1.** Whose heads bump on the sky?

The tall people's heads bump on the sky.

page 81   **2.** Whose ball lands in the sky?

_____

page 83   **3.** Whose tall son hits his head on the sky?

_____

page 84   **4.** Whose idea is it to push up the sky?

_____

page 85   **5.** Whose antlers get caught in the sky?

_____

page 87   **6.** Who won't be able to hide in the sky?

_____

MORE Possessive Nouns

Think of three things in your home that belong to different people.

 Write one sentence for each thing. Use a possessive noun to tell who owns it.

Graphic Organizer: Problem-and-Solution Chart

Pushing Up the Sky

📖 **Review "Pushing Up the Sky."**

✏️ **Complete the problem-and-solution chart.**

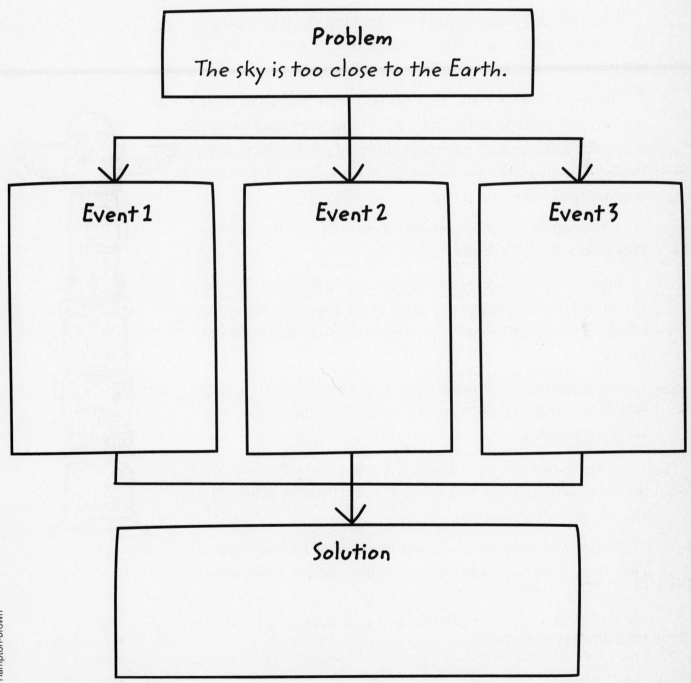

Problem
The sky is too close to the Earth.

Event 1

Event 2

Event 3

Solution

Identify Main Idea and Details

Read the passage below. Think about the main idea and the details.

Totem Poles

1   Many Native peoples in the past did not use written language. Some Native peoples of the Pacific Northwest used totem poles to tell their stories.

2   Totem poles were made from wood. People carved pictures into wooden poles to tell stories. No letters were used on the poles. The pictures were painted in different colors. Often, light shades of red, black, green, and blue were used. Sometimes brighter colors were added later.

3   Artists carved birds, fish, and other animals on totem poles to help them tell their stories.

4   Pictures were put in order on the totem pole and read from top to bottom. The story began at the top of the pole. It ended at the bottom of the pole. The main character of the story was always at the top.

5   Some stories on a totem pole told about special people. Sometimes, these people were still alive. Sometimes they were not alive anymore.

6   Other stories told about families. A pole called a Potlatch told about important events in a tribe's history. Potlatch poles were the tallest of all totem poles.

7   Totem poles were never repaired. They lasted for many years. Over time, their paint faded. Then people made new totem poles.

Now take the test on page 23.

Name _____ Date _____

Test Strategy

Look for words like *best* and *not*. They will help you find the correct answer choice.

Read each item. Choose the best answer.

1   The main idea of the passage is—

○   All totem poles were made from wood.

○   Some totem poles told stories about families.

○   Some Native peoples used totem poles to tell their stories.

○   Some artists carved animals on their totem poles.

2   Which detail does **not** support the main idea?

○   Some stories told about families.

○   A Potlatch pole is very tall.

○   Some stories on a totem pole told about special people.

○   People carved pictures into the wooden pole to tell a story.

3   Which detail **best** supports the main idea?

○   Totem poles were never repaired.

○   Over time, their paint faded.

○   Sometimes brighter colors were added later.

○   Pictures were put in order on the totem pole to tell the story.

4   Paragraph 2 is mostly about—

○   why totem poles were made.

○   how pictures were carved and painted.

○   the type of wood used for totem poles.

○   how tall some totem poles were.

Grammar: Common and Proper Nouns

What a Story!

 Read the paragraph carefully.

Many proper nouns are <u>not</u> capitalized correctly.

 Correct the capitalization of each proper noun.

> **Common and Proper Nouns**
>
> **Common nouns** name any person, place, or thing.
>
> **Proper nouns** name a particular person, place, or thing. Each important word in a proper noun is capitalized.

                                         B
I really enjoyed this story. The author, Joseph ƀruchac, is a great writer.

He is Native american and belongs to the abenaki tribe. The story is about a

different tribe called the snohomish. The Snohomish live by the ocean. My

favorite character in the story is seventh chief. He had a great idea to push

up the sky. My friend michael really liked the story, too. He used to live in

washington and saw some real totem poles. I am glad that my teacher,

mr. chan, read the story to our class.

MORE Common and Proper Nouns

In the paragraph above, circle all the common nouns.

Name _____ Date _____

Many Kinds of Homes

Key Words
frame
material
nation
Native peoples
permanent
region
temporary
traditional

 Work with a partner.

 Read each sentence.

 Write *T* for true. Write *F* for false.

T 1. You can use different **materials** to build a home.

_____ 2. A **region** is a kind of building.

_____ 3. A brick house is **temporary**.

_____ 4. Something that is **permanent** lasts for a long time.

_____ 5. Some **traditional** homes are made of mud.

_____ 6. Many **Native peoples** build homes with materials that are easy to find.

_____ 7. People in every **nation** live in homes of grass.

_____ 8. All homes are made with a wood **frame**.

MORE Key Words Practice

Walk around your neighborhood. Look at the homes. What different materials are they made of?

Write two sentences about the homes you see.

Name _____ Date _____

Where in the World?

👫 Work with a partner.

📖 Review "Native Homes."

✏️ Complete the chart. Write the names of regions, countries, and oceans you read about.

✔️ Check for capital letters.

Regions	Countries	Oceans
Eastern Woodlands	Canada	Pacific Ocean

MORE Common and Proper Nouns

✏️ Use your chart to write three sentences. Use one common noun and one proper noun in each sentence. Use capital letters for all proper nouns.

For use with TE p. T103

Name _____ Date _____

How Many Things?

👓 **What things do you see?**

✏️ **Write each answer. Be sure to make it plural by adding -s or -es.**

1. two _____*homes*_____
   home

2. many _____
   tree

3. some _____
   shoe

4. three _____
   box

5. four _____
   pole

6. three _____
   bush

7. some _____
   fox

8. two _____
   rug

9. five _____
   pot

10. four _____
    doll

© Hampton-Brown

Grammar: Plural Nouns

The Make-It-Plural Game

How to Play
The Make-It-Plural Game
· ·

1. Play with a partner. 🏃🏃

2. Spin the spinner for a singular noun (a noun that names one thing).

3. Change the noun to a plural noun (a noun that names more than one thing).

4. Make up sentences using the plural noun. 🖊 Write as many sentences as you can in five minutes.

Rules for Plurals

- If a noun ends in a **vowel** plus **y**, just add **-s** to form the plural.

  d<u>a</u>**y** ⟶ day**s**

- If a noun ends in a **consonant** plus **y**, change the **y** to **i**, then add **-es**.

  stor<u>y</u> ⟶ stor**ies**

Make a Spinner

1. Get a brad 🗲 and a large paper clip. ⎯⊃

2. Push the brad through the center of the circle.

3. Open the brad. ✏

4. Hook the paper clip over the brad to make a spinner.

© Hampton-Brown

Vocabulary Skill

Multiple-Meaning Words

 Read the meanings for each word.

Then read each sentence that uses the word.
Look for clues that tell you the meaning of the word.

Write the letter of the meaning that best fits each sentence.

Suit
A. A set of clothes with a jacket and pants or skirt
B. To go well with

_B_ **1.** These plankhouses **suit** the surrounding area.

_____ **2.** That **suit** is made of nice blue cloth.

Hide
A. The skin of an animal
B. To put something where no one sees it

_____ **3.** I will **hide** the presents behind the sofa so she can't find them.

_____ **4.** That tipi is made with buffalo **hide**.

Fire
A. Something burning; a flame
B. To shoot a gun or rifle

_____ **5.** In a tipi, the beds are arranged around the hot **fire**.

_____ **6.** The man learned how to **fire** a gun to hunt for food.

Safe
A. Not dangerous
B. A strong metal box, often used to hold money

_____ **7.** It is **safe** to build a fire in a tipi.

_____ **8.** The bank has a big **safe** in the back room.

Name _____ Date _____

Can You Count It?

 Read each sentence.

🖉 If the sentence is correct, write CORRECT.
   If the sentence is not correct, rewrite it correctly.

> ### Count and Non-Count Nouns
>
> Nouns that you can count have a singular and a plural form.
>
> Nouns that you cannot count have the same form for "one" and "more than one."

1. Some Native people grew **corns**.

   Some Native people grew corn.

2. They also grew different **bean**.

   _____

3. The crops were planted in the **soils**.

   _____

4. Many buffalo **hide** were used to build the tipi.

   _____

5. The men went to the forest to peel the **barks** off trees.

   _____

6. The **poles** were tied together to make the roof of a house.

   _____

7. Some houses were made of **muds**.

   _____

8. Some villages had several **longhouses** surrounded by a wooden wall.

   _____

For use with TE p. T117

Graphic Organizer: Comparison Chart

Native Homes

📖 Review "Native Homes."

✏️ Complete the comparison chart.

Kind of Home	Permanent or Temporary	Location	Materials
Longhouse	permanent	Northeast woods	wood, bark
Woven Grass Home			
Thatched Home			
Tipi			
Pueblo			
Plankhouse			

© Hampton-Brown

Name _____ Date _____

Make a Map

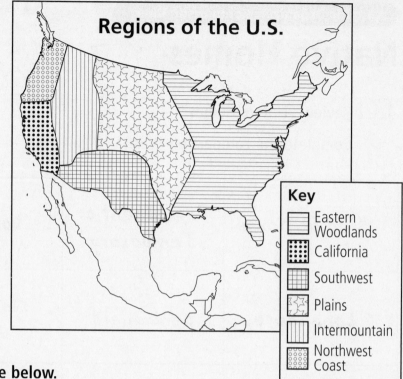

Regions of the U.S.

Key
- Eastern Woodlands
- California
- Southwest
- Plains
- Intermountain
- Northwest Coast

How to Make a Map

- Copy or trace an outline map of the area you are studying.

- Add the features you are interested in. Use symbols to save space.

- Add a map key to show what the symbols mean.

 Draw your own map in the space below.

Show the main rivers, lakes, and cities of your area.

Name _____ Date _____

A Land of Food

Look at the picture and read the paragraph.

Write the correct plural form of the word below the blank.

Rules for Plurals

- To make most nouns plural, add **-s**.
  home ⟶ home**s**

- If the noun ends in **x, ch, sh, s,** or **z**, add **-es**.
  branch ⟶ branch**es**

- For most nouns that end in **y**, change the **y** to **i** and add **-es**.
  sk~~y~~ ⟶ sk**ies**

- Some nouns cannot be counted. They have only one form.
  soil   rain   corn

Native peoples ate many different foods. They ate

_____ that grew on _____. They also ate
blueberry   bush

_____ that grew on _____. Some Native
squash   vine

peoples lived near the ocean. They used _____
net

or spears to catch fish like cod and salmon. Other people

planted crops like beans, _____, and potatoes.
corn

MORE Plural Nouns

Draw a picture and write a paragraph about your favorite foods.

Read your work to a partner.

Name _____   Date _____

Make a Flow Chart

 Fill in the flow chart. Write the steps you follow to make your favorite sandwich. You don't have to use all the boxes.

How to Make a Sandwich

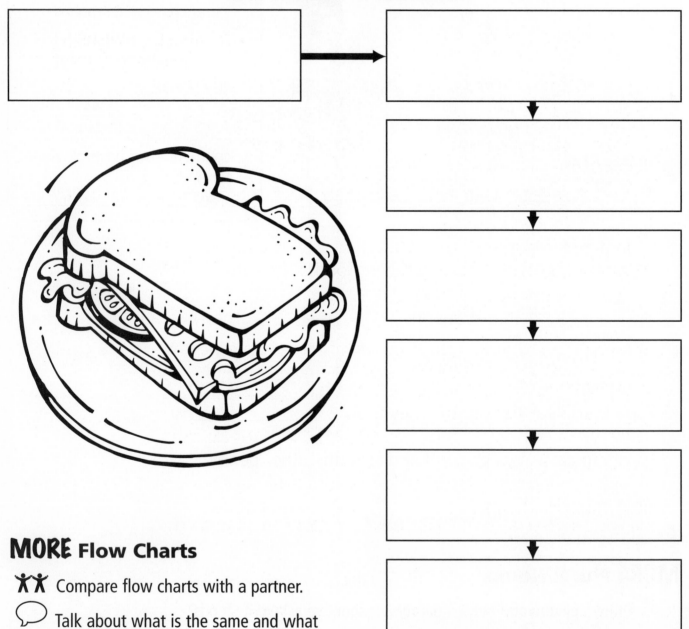

MORE Flow Charts

Compare flow charts with a partner.

Talk about what is the same and what is different.

© Hampton-Brown

Name _____ Date _____

Vocabulary: Key Words

Here Comes a Storm!

Key Words
cellar
damage
hail
howling
lightning
silent
thunder
twister

Name each picture. Use a Key Word.

1.

_____cellar_____

2.

_____

3.

_____

4.

_____

 Read each sentence.

✏️ **Circle the word that completes the sentence correctly. Then write the sentence.**

5. The ____(howling)/ silent____ of the wind scares my little brother.

   The howling of the wind scares my little brother.

6. A big storm can do a lot of ____cellar / damage____ to houses.

   _____

7. I always listen for ____thunder / cellar____ after I see lightning.

   _____

8. After the storm passes, everything gets ____twister / silent____.

   _____

Grammar: Action Verbs

The Action Game

Use these spinners to play The Action Game. The directions are on page 37.

Make the Spinners

1. Get a brad 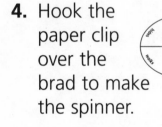 and a large paper clip.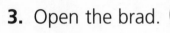

2. Push the brad through the center of the circle.

3. Open the brad.

4. Hook the paper clip over the brad to make the spinner.

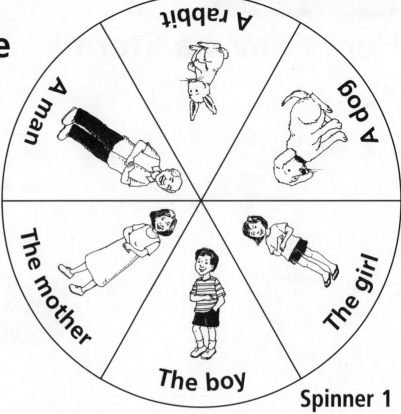

Spinner 1

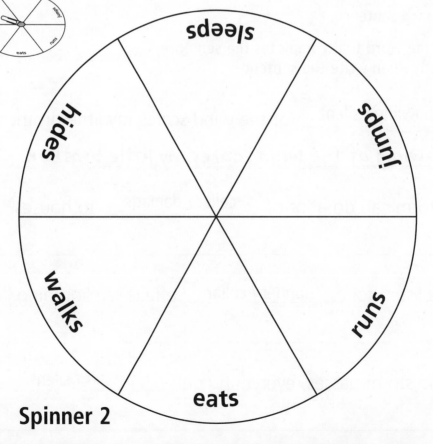

Spinner 2

Name _____ Date _____

The Action Game

How to Play The Action Game
• •

1. Play with a partner. 🏃🏃 Make the spinners from page 36.

2. Spin Spinner 1. ✏️ Write the words from Spinner 1 on the first line.

3. Spin Spinner 2. ✏️ Write the word next to the words you wrote from Spinner 1.

4. ✏️ Complete the sentence.

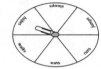

1. ____*A dog*____ ____*hides*____ ____*under the bed*____ .
     Spinner 1   Spinner 2

5. Read the sentence to your partner. 🏃🏃

6. Take turns.

7. ✏️ Write six sentences.

1. _____ _____ _____ .
    Spinner 1   Spinner 2

2. _____ _____ _____ .
    Spinner 1   Spinner 2

3. _____ _____ _____ .
    Spinner 1   Spinner 2

4. _____ _____ _____ .
    Spinner 1   Spinner 2

5. _____ _____ _____ .
    Spinner 1   Spinner 2

6. _____ _____ _____ .
    Spinner 1   Spinner 2

Name _____ Date _____

They Play Together

 Study the Rules for Subjects and Verbs.

Then read each sentence.

 **Write a verb in each blank.**

Rules for Subjects and Verbs

Action verbs that tell about one person or thing end in **-s**.

The boy **runs**.

Action verbs that tell about more than one person or thing don't end in **-s**.

The boys **run**.

---

1. Lucille _____ on the porch swing.
        sit / sits

2. The porch swing _____ on two chains.
        hang / hangs

3. The boy _____ a frozen fruit bar.
        lick / licks

4. He _____ in a wheelbarrow.
        ride / rides

5. The children _____ together outside.
        play / plays

6. Flowers _____ in Mr. Lyle's garden.
        grow / grows

7. Mr. Lyle _____ "Say hey!" to the children.
        shout / shouts

8. Raindrops _____ from the sky.
        fall / falls

9. Water drops _____ the roof of the house.
        hit / hits

---

10. Thunder _____ the small windows.
shake / shakes

11. Bird feeders _____ in the wind.
move / moves

12. A rabbit _____ across the grass.
run / runs

MORE Subject-Verb Agreement

📖 Find five sentences with action verbs in the story.
Do they tell about one person or thing, or about more than one?

✏️ Write each sentence, underline the verb, and
mark (✔) **One** or **More than One**. 🧍🧍

Page	Sentence	One	More than One
37	We <u>tap</u> our toes in puddles.		✔

Grammar: Subject-Verb Agreement

Here It Is! There They Are!

Here is/are; There is/are

- Use **here is** or **there is** to talk about one thing.

- Use **here are** or **there are** to talk about more than one thing.

 Look at the picture.

🖉 Write *Here is*, *Here are*, *There is*, or *There are* to complete each sentence.

1. _____Here_____ _____is_____ a house with a porch.

2. _____There_____ _____are_____ flowers in the yard.

3. _____ _____ three rabbits in the flowers.

4. _____ _____ an airplane high up in the air.

5. _____ _____ a porch swing.

6. _____ _____ two children on the lawn.

7. _____ _____ a man waving to the children.

8. _____ _____ two clouds in the sky.

9. _____ _____ a dog with the children.

10. _____ _____ two birds in the tree.

Graphic Organizer: Story Map

Twister

📖 Review "Twister."

✏️ Complete the story map.

Beginning
Lucille and Natt play outside. It begins to rain.
They run inside the house.

↓

Middle
1. A tornado comes toward the house.
2. Lucille, Natt, and Mama run to the cellar.
3.

4.

↓

End

Comprehension Skill

Summarize

Read the story below. Think about how to summarize it.

A Stormy Day

1   Alyssa sat in her classroom at school. She stared out the windows. Dark clouds formed in the sky. Raindrops began to splash against the window. Alyssa could hear the wind howl.

2   Alyssa's teacher told the students, "Go straight home after school. A big storm is coming!"

3   Alyssa started to walk home. Then she saw her friends, Cory and Marcia, jumping in puddles. "What fun!" Alyssa cried. The three friends danced in the puddles until the rain fell harder.

4   "Oh no!" Marcia said. "We'd better go home."

5   Alyssa hurried home and walked into the dark kitchen. She tried to turn on the lights. Nothing happened. Then she saw a shadow in the doorway.

6   Her dad walked into the kitchen. He was carrying a flashlight and some candles. He said, "The wind is very strong. The lights might not work until tomorrow."

7   Alyssa's mom said, "Let's sit by the fireplace. We can tell stories." The storm grew louder as Alyssa listened to her mother. She heard tree branches crack. The wind pounded against the windows. "I will be glad when this storm ends!" Alyssa said.

8   At last she fell asleep. It was very quiet when she woke up. The storm was over. Alyssa went outside to see the damage. Two trees were on the ground. A broken mailbox lay on the porch.

9   At school, everyone talked about the big storm. They were happy that the weather was clear and sunny again.

Now take the test on page 43.

Test Strategy
Read the directions carefully.
Make sure you understand
what to do.

Read each item. Choose the best answer.

1 Which of these sentences belongs in a summary of this story?

⬭ She heard tree branches crack.

⬭ A storm began while Alyssa was at school.

⬭ Rain began to splash on the window.

⬭ Her dad walked into the kitchen.

2 Which of the following completes this summary of the whole story?

> Alyssa was at school. The teacher told the students that a big storm was coming. Alyssa started to walk home. _____
>
> _____
>
> _____

⬭ She saw some of her friends. They played and danced in puddles. When the rain fell harder, they decided to go home. Alyssa's house was dark.

⬭ At home, Alyssa listened to her mother tell stories. She heard tree branches crack outside. The wind pounded against the windows. She fell asleep.

⬭ She stopped to play in some puddles. When the rain fell harder she went home. Her family sat by the fireplace and talked. The storm was over in the morning. The kids at Alyssa's school talked about it.

⬭ She went into the dark kitchen. Her dad came into the room. He had candles and a flashlight. He said, "The wind is very strong." Alyssa wished the storm would end.

Name _____ Date _____

Analyze a Character

Choose a character from "Twister." Complete the character map.

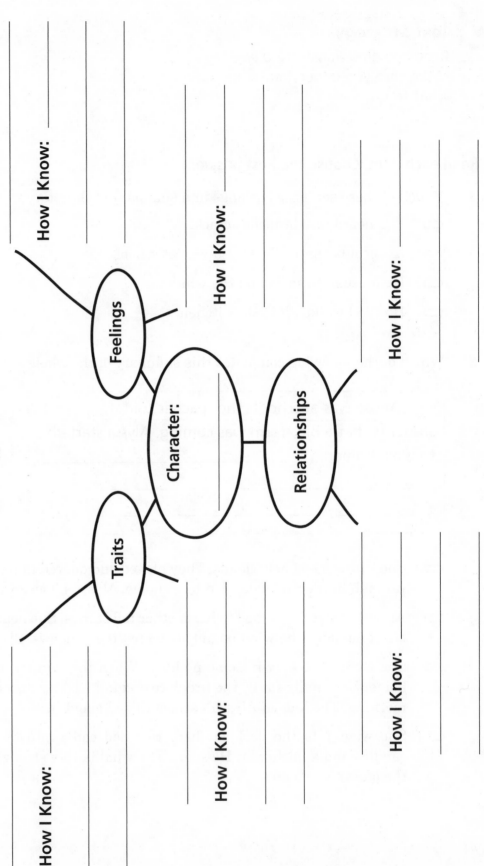

Feelings

How I Know: _____

How I Know: _____

Character: _____

Relationships

How I Know: _____

Traits

How I Know: _____

How I Know: _____

How I Know: _____

Name _____ Date _____

Bad Weather

You don't have to be a forecaster to know that weather is different in summer and winter! What dangerous weather do you get in your part of the country?

 Complete the chart. Use as many Key Words as possible. Add other weather words.

Key Words
blizzard
cold front
dangerous
forecaster
mass
temperature
thunderstorm
tornado

Dangerous Weather!

☀ In Summer	❄ In Winter
tornado	blizzard

Name _____ Date _____

It Is a Beautiful Day!

 Read the story.

 Write *is* or *are* in each blank.

 Draw the rest of the picture.

It _____ a beautiful summer day. The sky _____ blue.

Two houses _____ on a hill. A long stream _____ next to

the hill. Many fish _____ in the stream. They _____

near a big rock. A girl _____ on the rock. A boy

_____ in the stream. He _____ a

good swimmer. Four birds _____ in a tree.

They sing beautifully. We _____

happy that the sun _____

in the sky. What a beautiful day!

MORE Subject-Verb Agreement

Think about a rainy or snowy day.

 Write about that day. Use *is* and *are*.

 Draw a picture of the day. Share your work with a partner. 🏃🏃

Multiple-Meaning Words

 Read each sentence.

Then read the two meanings of the word in dark print.

 Circle the letter of the correct meaning of the word in the sentence. Write what clues helped you figure out the meaning.

1. The warm air **flows** quickly from the Gulf of Mexico.

   A. To move along in a stream

   B. To hang loosely

   _____

2. The **date** of the big storm was March 31, 1982.

   A. A sweet fruit that grows on a palm tree

   B. The time when something happens

   _____

3. The dark clouds are a **sign** that it will rain later.

   A. A clue that something is going to happen

   B. A board or poster that gives information

   _____

4. Today's freezing temperature was a **record**!

   A. A report that is written down

   B. The highest or lowest mark

   _____

Name _____ Date _____

We Have Many Kinds of Weather

 Look at the map. Read the description.

Write *has* or *have* in each blank to complete the description.

We _____ many different kinds of weather in the United

States. Some states _____ a lot of snow in winter. Vermont

_____ snow every year. Other states do not _____

snow at all. Arizona _____ very hot weather. Washington

_____ very rainy weather. Tornadoes can happen all across the

United States. The southern states _____ a lot of tornadoes in the

spring. The northern states _____ many tornadoes in the summer.

© Hampton-Brown

Graphic Organizer: Time Line

The Big Storm

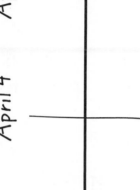 Review "The Big Storm."

Complete the time line.

1982

March 31   April 1   April 2   April 3   April 4   April 5   April 6

California
rain and
snow

Rocky
Mountains
blizzards

Research Skill

Make an Outline

How to Make an Outline

- Write a title that tells your research topic.

- List your main ideas with roman numerals.

- Under each main idea, write details. Use capital letters for each important detail. Use numbers for each smaller detail.

Types of Clouds

I. Fair Weather Clouds
  A. Cumulus clouds
    1. puffy white clouds
    2. have flat bottoms
  B. Stratus clouds
    1. form in layers
    2. cover large areas of the sky
II. Bad Weather Clouds

✂ **Cut out the parts of an outline.**

Put the parts in order to form a correct outline.

Paste or tape them on a separate sheet of paper.

B. Snow	**I.** Summer
C. Large hail	**B.** Tornadoes
2. lightning and thunder	**1.** wind and rain
1. winds of 180 miles per hour	Bad Weather in the Midwest
II. Winter	**2.** funnel-shaped clouds
A. Thunderstorms	**A.** Very cold temperatures

Name _____ Date _____

Grammar: Subject-Verb Agreement

They Play in the Snow

 Study the Rules for Verbs. Then read each sentence.

✏ Write the correct verb in each blank.

Rules for Verbs

When you talk about one person or thing, use *is* or add **-s** to an action verb.

The girl **smiles**.
She **is** happy.

When you talk about more than one person or thing, use **are** or use an action verb without **-s**.

The girls **smile**.
They **are** happy.

---

1. Wanda _____ in the snow.
    dance / dances

2. Her brother _____ excited to build a snowman.
    is / are

3. It is too cold! They _____ into the house.
    run / runs

4. Jim _____ into dry clothes.
    change / changes

5. Wanda _____ her coat on a hook.
    hang / hangs

6. The children _____ happy to be in a warm house.
    is / are

MORE Subject-Verb Agreement

👥 Ask two partners about the kinds of weather they like.

✏ Write a sentence about a type of weather each of them likes.

Then write a sentence about a type of weather they both like.

Name _____ Date _____

Use a Glossary

 Study the glossary page. Then read each sentence.

 Write *T* if the sentence is true. Write *F* if the sentence is false.

---

arctic (**ark**-tik) *adjective* The **arctic** region is a very cold area around the North Pole. *Arctic air masses bring very low temperatures.*

cumulus (**kyūm**-yū-lus) *adjective* A **cumulus** cloud is white and fluffy with a flat bottom. *The cumulus clouds float in the sky.*

downpour (**down**-por) *noun* A **downpour** is a heavy fall of rain. *The boy got very wet in the downpour.*

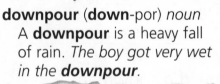

drought (drowt) *noun* A **drought** is a long period of time without rain. *The animals could not find enough water to drink during the drought.*

evaporation (i-**vap**-u-**rā**-shun) *noun* **Evaporation** is when a liquid changes into a gas. From **vapor**. *The evaporation of the rain took many hours.*

hail (hāl) *noun* **Hail** is small, round pieces of ice that fall to earth like rain or snow. *During the storm, hail hit the ground like little rocks.*

_____ 1. *Hail* rhymes with *mile*.

_____ 2. The picture of the rain goes with the entry for **drought**.

_____ 3. A word in dark print, like *arctic*, is called an **entry word**.

_____ 4. Arctic weather is good for going to the beach.

_____ 5. *Evaporation* comes from the root word *vapor*.

_____ 6. There are a lot of downpours during a drought.

_____ 7. *Drought* rhymes with *out.*

_____ 8. In evaporation, water becomes ice.

_____ 9. Cumulus clouds are a sign of bad weather.

_____ 10. Hail is small, round pieces of earth.

Vocabulary: Key Words

The Mysterious Friend

Key Words
backward
boldness
capture
curious
discover
mysterious
promise
secret

👓 **Read the story.**

✏️ **Circle the word that completes each sentence correctly.**

I like to know about eveything. I am very

___curious / boldness___ about the world. Today, my

___discover / boldness___ almost caused some trouble. I wanted to

___discover / secret___ something about the new girl next door.

I did not know anything about her. She seemed very ___capture / mysterious___

to me.

There is a hole in the fence between our houses. No one else knows

about this ___promise / secret___ hole. I looked through the hole, and

someone was looking back at me! I nearly fell ___backward / curious___ away

from the hole. The girl said, "Let's ___promise / backward___ never to do that

again." Then the girl yelled, "Try to ___mysterious / capture___ me if you can!"

Now I know something about the girl. She runs fast!

MORE Key Words Practice

💬 Tell a partner about something you are curious about.

Vocabulary Skill

Prefixes *un-, dis-, re-*

👓 **Study the Prefix Chart. Then read each sentence.**

✏️ **Write the correct prefixed word to complete each sentence.**

Prefix Chart

A **prefix** is a word part that comes at the beginning of a word. A prefix changes a word's meaning.

Prefix	Meaning	Example
dis-	"the opposite of"	discover
un-	"not"	unkind
re-	"again" or "back"	return

---

1. Leon _____*rechecks*_____ Paco's "secret message" on the computer.

checks again

2. Paco lives on an island, _____ Leon, who lives in the city.

not like

3. Leon wants to _____ Paco's island home.

visit again

4. He is _____ that his friend lives so far away.

not happy

5. Leon's parents think it is _____ for him to go alone.

not safe

6. They _____ the idea of Leon going far away.

the opposite of "like"

7. Leon _____ with his parents.

the opposite of "agrees"

8. He thinks it is _____ that he can't go!

not fair

9. Paco says people on the island _____ stories from long ago.

tell again

10. Leon wants to _____ how it feels to live on an island.

the opposite of "cover"

Grammar: Sensory Adjectives

A Wonderful Place

 Write a paragraph that describes your favorite place.

Use adjectives from the box, or choose some of your own.

Try to use at least one adjective for each of the senses.

Share your work with a partner.

Sensory Adjectives

Sight	Sound	Taste	Feel	Smell
blue	quiet	sweet	soft	fresh
large	loud	salty	sharp	sweet
round	soft	sour	cold	smoky
dark	silent	delicious	rough	perfumed
small	noisy	spicy	smooth	aromatic

_____

_____

_____

_____

_____

_____

_____

_____

_____

Name _____ Date _____

Some Shells for Sale!

 Look at the picture. Read each sentence.

 Complete each sentence. Write a number word or an adjective like *some*, *several*, or *many*.

1. The man wears _____ shell around his neck.

2. The baskets hold _____ shells.

3. _____ shells are on the pole.

4. _____ people are on the sand.

5. The box has _____ shells on its top.

6. There are _____ palm trees behind the shell shop.

7. There are _____ clouds in the sky.

MORE Adjectives That Tell How Many

XX Tell your partner more about what you see at the shop and on the beach. Use number words or ***some***, ***several***, or ***many*** to talk about what you see.

Graphic Organizer: Character Chart

The Secret Footprints

📖 Review "The Secret Footprints."   ✏️ Complete the character chart.

	Actions	Motives
pages 210–212	1. Guapa goes out before it is dark.	She is curious.
page 213	2. Guapa goes too close to the house.	
pages 214–215	3.	
pages 216–217	4.	
pages 218–219	5.	
pages 220–221	6.	
pages 222–223	7.	
pages 224–227	8.	
page 228	9.	
pages 229–230	10.	

Vocabulary Strategy

Read Long Words

Read the story below. Think about how to read long words.

Oolah the Oyster

1   Oolah was an oyster. She was in her usual place. She was at the edge of the big rock near the sandy beach. Her brother Gloog was with her. They watched two humans eat lunch on the beach.

2   Oolah said, "The humans will throw their garbage in the water. They think that is acceptable!"

3   Gloog sighed, "Trash is harmful to every creature in the ocean." Gloog thought about the way oysters breathe and eat. They breathe water instead of air. They breathe with their gills, like fish.

4   Oysters drink ocean water. They eat animals and plants in the ocean. Then they spit the water back into the ocean.

5   Gloog was angry. Any garbage in the water would mix with their food. It is so careless to throw trash in the ocean! His heart started to beat faster.

6   "I must protect us," he said. "We're not defenseless! I'm sure there is something we can do. Oolah, I don't understand human language. Tell me what the people are saying."

7   Oolah listened as the two humans talked. Then she said, "It's okay, Gloog! They seem grateful for the beautiful ocean. The woman said that dirty water hurts the fish and makes them sick. The man said that everyone should be thoughtful about the animals in the ocean."

Now take the test on page 59.

Name _____ Date _____

 Test Strategy
Skip an item if you're not sure
of the answer. Come back to it
later. Make your best guess.

Read each item. Choose the best answer.

1   Read the first sentence in paragraph 3 on page 58.
What does the word <u>harmful</u> mean?

- ⬭ not bad
- ⬭ with care
- ⬭ full of harm
- ⬭ without harm

2   Read the second sentence in paragraph 6 on page 58.
The word <u>defenseless</u> means—

- ⬭ full of defense
- ⬭ without defense
- ⬭ with great defense
- ⬭ with very little defense

3   Read paragraph 2 on page 58.
If it is <u>acceptable</u> to throw trash, that means—

- ⬭ it can be accepted
- ⬭ it is not good to do
- ⬭ it cannot be accepted
- ⬭ it has to be done often

4   In paragraph 5, what does the word <u>careless</u> mean?

- ⬭ with care
- ⬭ without care
- ⬭ full of care
- ⬭ with much care

Vocabulary Skill

Figurative Language

 Read each sentence. Look for the simile.

 Use plain language to rewrite each sentence.

> A **simile** is a comparison that uses the word **as** or **like**.
>
> The ciguapas' caves were **as** blue **as** the sky.
>
> Guapa's skin was **like** gold.

1. Guapa was as bold as a lioness.

Guapa was fearless.

2. The sunset is as colorful as a rainbow.

_____

3. The stars are like diamonds in the sky.

_____

4. The boy ran like a speeding train.

_____

 Read each sentence.

Use a simile to rewrite the sentence.

5. The palm trees moved in the breeze.

The palm trees swayed like dancers in the breeze.

6. The *pastelitos* taste sweet.

_____

7. The sand feels soft.

_____

For use with TE pp. T237a–T237b

Name _____ Date _____

Words Under the Sea

Key Words
backbone
blend
camouflage
creature
deadly
defense
safety
shelter

Read each sentence.

Rewrite each sentence. Replace the word or words in dark print with a Key Word.

1. Jun adds a new **animal** to her fish tank.

Jun adds a new creature to her fish tank.

2. The anemone has no **bones along its back**.

_____

3. Some sea animals use **a special way to hide** to keep safe.

_____

4. Their colors **match** with the colors around them.

_____

5. The anemone's stingers are its **protection** from danger.

_____

6. Its **killing** stingers do not harm some animals.

_____

7. Clownfish can find **a place to live** inside the anemone's arms.

_____

8. The anemone's stingers give clownfish **freedom from danger**.

_____

Name _____ Date _____

Into the Sea!

📖 **Look at the page in "Hello, Fish!"**

✏️ **Write a preposition to complete each sentence.**

✔️ **Check your work with a partner.** 🧍🧍

> **Use of Prepositions**
>
> Prepositions introduce phrases that tell more about something.
>
> Fish swim. ⟶ Fish swim **in** *the water.*
>
> Here are some common prepositions:
>
> in   from   with   on   into   for

📖 **page 242**   **1.** Fish have fins to help them swim ___*through*___ the water.
                                                    above / through

📖 **page 243**   **2.** Many fish live _____ coral reefs.
                                    around / before

📖 **page 245**   **3.** Morays may remind you _____ curious kittens.
                                        of / on

📖 **page 247**   **4.** Clownfish coat their fins _____ goo.
                                        about / with

📖 **page 248**   **5.** A scorpionfish blends in _____ colorful sponges.
                                        against / from

📖 **page 251**   **6.** A brown goby dives _____ its shelter for safety.
                                    with / into

📖 **page 252**   **7.** Frogfish look around _____ big eyes.
                                    with / on

📖 **page 254**   **8.** Sharks have lived _____ a long time.
                                    of / for

MORE Prepositions

✏️ Write a paragraph about creatures of the sea. Use prepositions to begin phrases that tell more about each creature.

Name _____ Date _____

The Warmest Water

 Read the Rule Box. Look at the pictures.

✏️ **Complete each sentence. Add *-er* or *-est* to the word below the line.**

Adjectives That Compare

- To compare two things, add **-er**:
  The water in Astoria is **warmer** than the water in Eastport.

- To compare more than two things, add **-est**:
  The water in Baltimore is the **warmest** of these three cities.

Eastport, Maine	Astoria, Oregon	Baltimore, Maryland

warm	**warmer**	**warmest**

Baltimore, Maryland	**Eastport, Maine**	**Miami Beach, Florida**	**Astoria, Oregon**
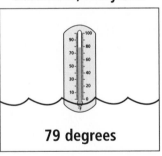	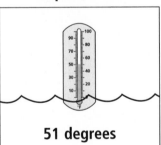	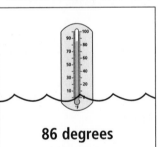	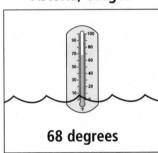
79 degrees	**51 degrees**	**86 degrees**	**68 degrees**

1. Baltimore's water is _____*warmer*_____ than Astoria's water.
　　　　　　　　　　　　　　warm

2. Miami Beach's water is _____ than Eastport's water.
　　　　　　　　　　　　　　　warm

3. Eastport has the _____ water of all the cities.
　　　　　　　　　　　cold

4. Astoria's water is _____ than the water in Miami Beach.
　　　　　　　　　　　cold

5. Miami Beach has the _____ water of all the cities.
　　　　　　　　　　　　warm

Name _____ Date _____

The Longest Reefs

 Look at the pictures.

 Complete each sentence. Add *-er* or *-est* to the word below the line.

Philippine Reefs	**Bahamian Archipelago Reefs**	**Red Sea Reefs**	**Reefs of the Pacific Atolls**

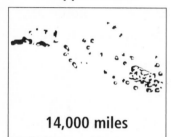   

14,000 miles	1,000 miles	3,000 miles	17,000 miles

1. The Reefs of the Pacific Atolls are the _____*longest*_____ reefs.

               long

2. The Philippine Reefs are _____ than the Red Sea Reefs.

            long

3. The Red Sea Reefs are _____ than the Reefs of the Pacific Atolls.

        short

4. The Bahamian Archipelago Reefs are _____ than the Philippine Reefs.

            short

5. The Bahamian Archipelago Reefs are the _____ reefs.

            short

MORE Adjectives That Compare

 Find four classmates of different heights.

 Write four sentences about them on a separate sheet of paper. Use *shorter*, *shortest*, *taller*, and *tallest*.

Name _____ Date _____

Least Favorite, Most Popular!

Popular Beach Activities

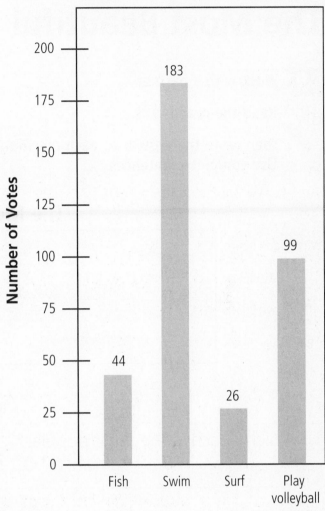

Comparisons

To compare with longer adjectives:

- use **more** or **less** to compare two things
- use **most** or **least** to compare three or more things

Do not add **-er** or **-est** to long adjectives.

 Read the graph.

 Work with a partner.

Write the answer to each question. Use complete sentences.

1. What is the most popular thing to do at the beach?

   The most popular thing to do is swim.

2. What is the least popular thing to do at the beach?

   _____

   _____

3. What is more popular: to play volleyball or to fish?

   _____

   _____

Name _____   Date _____

The Most Beautiful Beach!

  Work with a partner.

Read the graph.

Then write the answer to each question.
Use complete sentences.

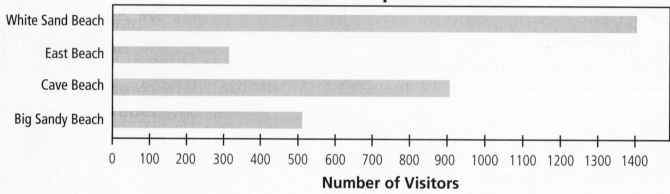

The Most Popular Beaches

Number of Visitors

1. Which beach is the most popular?

   _____

2. Which beach is the least popular?

   _____

3. Which beach is more popular than Cave Beach?

   _____

MORE Comparisons

Talk to a partner about sea creatures you have read about.
Which creature is the most unusual or the least unusual?
Which is the most interesting or the least interesting?

Write three sentences to compare these sea creatures.

Name _____ Date _____

Graphic Organizer: Cluster

Hello, Fish!

 Review "Hello, Fish!"

🖉 **Complete the cluster.**

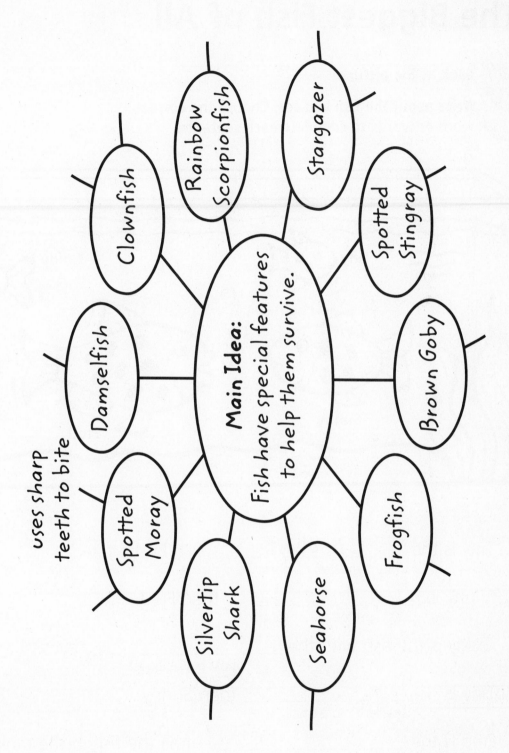

uses sharp
teeth to bite

Damselfish

Clownfish

Rainbow
Scorpionfish

Stargazer

Spotted
Stingray

Main Idea:
Fish have special features
to help them survive.

Brown Goby

Spotted
Moray

Silvertip
Shark

Seahorse

Frogfish

Name _____ Date _____

The Biggest Fish of All

 Look at the picture.

 Write about the fish you see. Choose the correct word or words to complete each sentence.

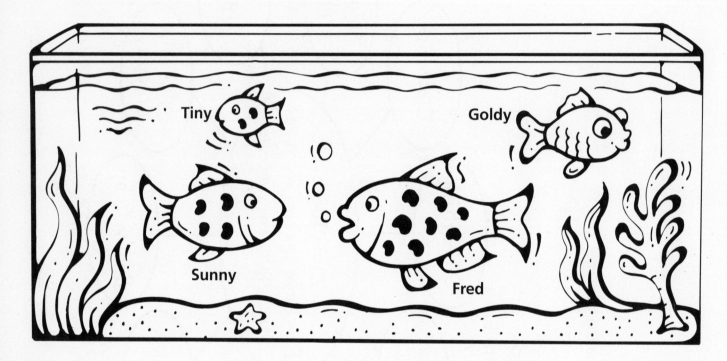

1. Tiny is the _____*smallest*_____ fish in the tank.
smallest / biggest

2. Sunny is _____ than Fred.
less spotted / least spotted

3. Goldy is the fish with the _____ eyes.
most big / biggest

4. Tiny is _____ than Sunny.
smaller / more small

5. Fred is the _____ of all the fish in the tank.
more spotted / most spotted

6. Sunny is _____ than Goldy.
bigger / biggest

For use with TE pp. T262–T263

Vocabulary Skill

Use a Dictionary

👓 **Study this part of a page from a dictionary.**

Then follow the directions on page 70.

---

predator ➤ product

predator An animal that hunts and kills other animals for food: *Owls are forest predators.* **pred•a•tor** (**pred**-u-tur) *Noun.*

predict To tell what will happen in the future: *The weather report predicts rain for tomorrow.* **pre•dict** (pri-**dikt**) *Verb.*

preen 1. To clean the feathers with the beak, such as a bird does. **2.** To dress oneself neatly: *She preened herself before the party.* **preen** (prēn) *Verb.*

preserve To protect; keep safe: *We must preserve the animals that live in the ocean. Verb.*
○ A place where wild animals, plants, or fish can live safely: *We visited a tiger preserve on our vacation. Noun.*
pre•serve (pri-**zurv**) *Verb; Noun.*

press 1. To push against or squeeze with force: *Please press the doorbell.* **2.** To make clothes smooth with an iron: *I need to press my shirt.* **3.** To crowd together: *We pressed into the tiny room. Verb.*
○ All the newspapers and magazines and the people who work for them: *The members of the press waited for an interview. Noun.*
press (pres) *Verb; Noun.*

pretend 1. To make believe: *I like to pretend that I can fly.* **2.** To make someone believe something that is not true: *He telephoned the school, pretending to be sick.*
pre•tend (pri-**tend**) *Verb.*

prey 1. An animal that is hunted and eaten by another animal: *Mice are often the prey of cats.* **2.** A person or thing that is helpless against trouble: *The small boy was the prey of the town bully. Noun.*
○ To hunt other animals for food: *Tigers prey on smaller animals. Verb.*
prey (prā) *Noun; Verb.*

price The cost of something: *What is the price of that car? Noun.*
○ To set the price of something: *The owner priced the book at $50. Verb.*
price (prīs) *Noun; Verb.*

primate A member of the group of mammals that includes human beings, monkeys, and apes: *A chimpanzee is a primate.* **pri•mate** (**prī**-māt) *Noun.*

procedure A way or method to do something: *Please show me the correct procedure for changing a tire.*
pro•ce•dure (pru-**sē**-jur) *Noun.*

Vocabulary Skill

Use a Dictionary

👫 Work with a partner. Use the dictionary page from one book.
Use the questions page from the other book.

💬 Read a question to your partner. Your partner answers the
question. Take turns asking and answering questions.

✏️ Then write each answer in your own book.

1. What part of speech is **predict**?

   "Predict" is a verb.

2. Could the word **program** appear on this dictionary page? Explain your answer.

   _____

   _____

3. What does the word **predator** mean?

   _____

4. What word do you know that rhymes with **preen**?

   _____

5. Which entry word has the most definitions?

   _____

6. Which of the following sentences uses the word **price** as a noun?
   What is the price of this computer? Please do not price these cars too high!

   _____

7. Are all primates monkeys? Explain your answer.

   _____

A Special Trip

✏️ **Write a Key Word to complete each label.**

Key Words
arrive
bloom
emperor
forgot
lotus
remember
special
throne

1. _____

2. _____

3. _____

👓 **Read the paragraph.**

✏️ **Write the correct Key Word to complete each sentence.**

My family took a _____ trip last summer. We rushed
                        4. very important

to the airport because we needed to _____ early. I almost
                                           5. get there

_____ my camera. I am very glad my mom reminded me!
    6. did not think of

At a museum, I saw a painting of an emperor. He had a beautiful white

_____ in his hand. My mother said it was a lotus flower. Now,
      7. flower

I have my pictures to help me _____.
                                  8. think about the past

Grammar: Subject Pronouns

It Happened!

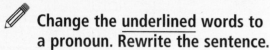 Look at the page in "The Lotus Seed."

Read the sentence on this page.

Change the underlined words to a pronoun. Rewrite the sentence.

> **Subject Pronouns**
>
> A **subject pronoun** takes the place of a noun in the subject of a sentence.
>
> | For | Use |
> |---|---|
> | one boy or man | he |
> | one girl or woman | she |
> | one thing | it |
> | more than one person or thing | they |

page 273　**1.** <u>A young girl</u> tells why a lotus seed is important to her.

She tells why a lotus seed is important to her.

page 274　**2.** <u>The emperor</u> lost his dragon throne.

_____

page 275　**3.** <u>The lotus seed</u> was wrapped in a piece of silk.

_____

page 276　**4.** <u>The mother-of-pearl hair combs</u> were on the floor.

_____

page 277　**5.** <u>Her children and cousins</u> all lived in one big house.

_____

page 279　**6.** <u>The little boy</u> planted the seed in a pool of mud.

_____

page 280　**7.** <u>The lotus flower</u> is the flower of life and hope.

_____

page 280　**8.** <u>The grandmother</u> gave each grandchild a seed.

_____

Name _____ Date _____

I Got a Special Gift

 Look at the picture. Read each sentence.

 Write the correct pronoun to complete each sentence.

Subject Pronouns

- Use *I* to tell about yourself.
- Use *we* to tell about yourself and another person or persons.
- Use *you* when you talk to another person or persons.

1.

__We__ are a family. _____ have a special gift for you.

Oh, Grandmother, _____ are so wonderful!

2.

Do _____ like the gift?

Yes, _____ love it!

3.

_____ both have the same necklace now.

_____ are very important to me.

_____ am happy to be your granddaughter!

Grammar: Possessive Pronouns

The Pronoun Game

How to Play The Pronoun Game

1. Play with a partner. 🧍🧍

2. Spin the spinner.

3. 📖 Open "The Lotus Seed" to the page or pages on the spinner.

👓 Look at the picture. Find a noun (a person, place, or thing).

4. ✏️ Make two sentences: one with the noun, and one with the noun and the possessive pronoun on the spinner.

   Example: *There is a seed.*
   Is it your seed?

5. ✏️ Write your sentences.

6. Read them to a partner. 🧍🧍

7. Take turns.

8. See how many sentences you and your partner can write in 15 minutes.

Make a Spinner

1. Get a brad 📌 and a large paper clip. 📎

2. Push the brad through the center of the circle.

3. Open the brad.

4. Hook the paper clip over the brad to make a spinner.

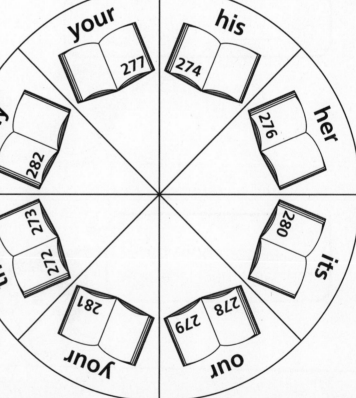

© Hampton-Brown

Graphic Organizer: Sequence Chain

The Lotus Seed

📖 **Review "The Lotus Seed."**

✏️ **Complete the sequence chain.**

Bà takes a lotus seed to help her remember the emperor.

↓

Bà gets married and carries the seed in her pocket for good luck.

↓

↓

↓

↓

↓

Draw Conclusions

Read the passage below. Think about how to draw conclusions.

Two Cultures, Two Friends

1   Jin came to the United States from Korea. The new way of life in America was hard for her. At first, Jin knew only a few English words. It was not easy for Jin to make friends. She could not understand what the other students said. She could not say what she wanted to say.

2   Another girl in Jin's class was from Korea, too. Her name was Cho. Cho came to this country a year ago. She helped Jin understand new words. She showed Jin many of the customs in the United States.

3   Cho and Jin talked about American culture and Korean culture. They laughed about how they were alike and different. It felt good to talk to someone who knew about both cultures.

4   In Korea, you take off your shoes when you visit someone at home. Here, many people wear their shoes at home. In Korea, people use both hands to give or accept a gift. This country does not follow that custom.

5   Jin did not eat the school lunches at first. She brought her lunch from home. Finally, Cho encouraged her to try the school lunches. Jin liked pizza and hamburgers. She and Cho still liked to bring their lunch from home a few days a week.

6   At the end of the school year, Jin thanked Cho for all her help. She told Cho, "You are a great friend." Cho smiled.

Now take the test on page 77.

Name _____ Date _____

Read each item. Choose the best answer.

1   Which detail helps you draw this conclusion: Jin and Cho had something in common.

   ⊂⊃   Jin liked pizza and hamburgers.

   ⊂⊃   Jin knew only a few English words.

   ⊂⊃   Jin could not say what she wanted to say.

   ⊂⊃   Jin and Cho knew about American and Korean culture.

2   What conclusion can you draw about Cho after reading the passage?

   ⊂⊃   Cho liked to help Jin.

   ⊂⊃   Cho didn't know much English.

   ⊂⊃   Cho will move back to Korea soon.

   ⊂⊃   Cho doesn't have any brothers or sisters.

3   Look at this diagram.

Detail: Jin didn't know much English.	+	Detail: Cho helped Jin understand new words.	=	Conclusion:

What is the best conclusion you can draw from these details?

   ⊂⊃   Jin still cannot speak English.

   ⊂⊃   Jin understands more English now.

   ⊂⊃   Jin likes to write stories in English.

   ⊂⊃   Jin does not watch much television.

Name _____ Date _____

Analyze Characters

Think of a character from another story in this book or from another book.

 Complete the trait chart for the character.

Character: _____

Story: _____

Traits	Clues from Story
	page _____
	page _____
	page _____
	page _____
	page _____

© Hampton-Brown

A Nation of Immigrants

👥 Work with one or more partners.

✏️ Complete the word web about immigrants.

Key Words
adjust
better future
come from
culture
opportunity
pride

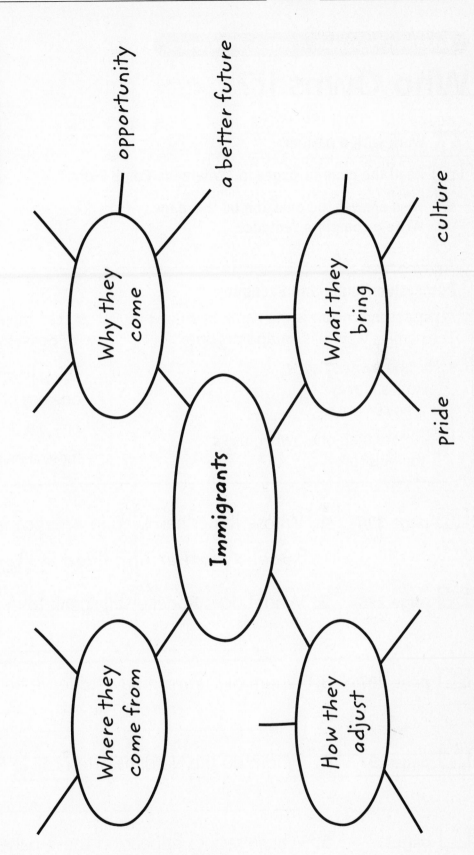

Why they come — opportunity, a better future

Immigrants

What they bring — culture, pride

Where they come from

How they adjust

Name _____   Date _____

Who Owns It?

 Work with a partner.

📖 Read the page or pages in "Where We Come From."

✏️ Then answer the question on this page.
Write a complete sentence.

Possessive Nouns and Pronouns

A **possessive noun** is the name of an owner. The name always has an **apostrophe**: **'**.

- For one owner, use **'s**.
  Ruth**'s** letters
  a boy**'s** books

- For more than one owner, use **s'**.
  the girl**s'** bikes

You can replace **possessive nouns** with **possessive pronouns**.

For	Use
one boy or man	his
one girl or woman	her
more than one person	their

📖 **page 296**   **1.** Whose father had lived in America for seven years?

Rogelio's father had lived in America for seven years.

📖 **page 296**   **2.** Whom does Rogelio still speak to in the Philippines?

_____

📖 **page 297**   **3.** Whom did Jasmine have to leave behind in El Salvador?

_____

📖 **page 297**   **4.** Whom do the Nardans often call in Fiji?

_____

📖 **pages 300–301**   **5.** Whose recipes appear on these pages?

_____

For use with TE p. T299b

Name _____ Date _____

A New Home for Us

 Find the page in "Where We Come From."

Review the page.

Change the underlined word or words to an object pronoun. Rewrite the sentence.

> **Object Pronouns**
>
> Use an **object pronoun** after an action verb or after a small word like *for* or *to*.
>
> | One | More than One |
> |---|---|
> | me | us |
> | you | you |
> | him, her, it | them |

page 296   **1.** The hardest thing for <u>Rogelio</u> was to learn English.

The hardest thing for him was to learn English.

page 296   **2.** Rogelio's father was lonely without <u>his family</u>.

_____

page 297   **3.** Jasmine talks with <u>her aunts</u> once a month.

_____

page 298   **4.** It made José sad to leave <u>grandparents, aunts, and uncles</u>.

_____

page 298   **5.** He rode around in <u>the car</u>.

_____

page 299   **6.** Charlotte's family brought <u>Charlotte</u> to America.

_____

page 299   **7.** Gabriel says, "My uncle told stories to <u>my brothers and me</u>."

_____

© Hampton-Brown

Graphic Organizer: Fact-and-Opinion Chart

Where We Come From

🖊 Review "Where We Come From." ✏ Complete the chart.

Person	Facts	Opinions	Opinion Signal Words
Rogelio Lorenzo III, Page 296	I came when I was seven years old. My grandparents still live there.	I miss my friends.	miss
Jasmine Aviles, Page 297			
Namita Nardan, Page 297			
José Villegas, Page 298			

✏ Now continue this chart on a separate sheet of paper. Tell about Charlotte Fale and Gabriel Balesteros.

© Hampton-Brown

Grammar: Pronouns

They Bring It with Them

 Read each sentence.

Replace the underlined words with the correct object pronoun.

Rewrite the sentence.

> **Object Pronouns**
>
> Use these pronouns after an **action verb** or a short word like *of*, *to*, or *with*.
>
> | One | More than One |
> |-----|---------------|
> | me | us |
> | you | you |
> | him, her, it | them |

1. Immigrants usually adjust quickly to <u>a new life</u>.

   Immigrants usually adjust quickly to it.

2. Rogelio calls <u>his cousin</u> in the Philippines.

   _____

3. Jasmine was sad to leave <u>family and friends</u> behind.

   _____

4. Namita does not remember <u>Fiji</u> very well.

   _____

5. José was surprised about <u>the fast cars</u>.

   _____

6. Immigrants bring <u>you and me</u> recipes from their cultures.

   _____

7. Give <u>my mother</u> a recipe for <u>Risi e Bisi</u>, please!

   _____

Name _____   Date _____

What Do They Eat?

 Read each sentence. Look at the underlined words.

Change the underlined words to pronouns.
Rewrite the sentence.

1. Mama gave Papa and me a recipe for Risi e Bisi.

   Mama gave us a recipe for Risi e Bisi.

2. Papa and I followed the directions carefully.

   _____

3. I stirred the chicken broth for fifteen minutes.

   _____

4. Papa let my sister add the rice.

   _____

5. My brother can help my cousins set the table.

   _____

6. My aunt helps Papa and me serve the food.

   _____

7. You must give the recipe to my uncle!

   _____

8. Risi e Bisi makes Papa think of Italy.

   _____

Name _____ Date _____

Vocabulary: Key Words

Contest Words

Key Words
contest
design
honor
sketch
talent

 Think of something you do well.

Read each incomplete sentence.

 Complete each sentence with your own words.

1. I have a special **talent** for

_____

_____

2. A **contest** I could win is

_____

_____

3. A person I want to **honor** is

_____

_____

4. I can think of a good **design** for

_____

_____

MORE Design Ideas

 On another sheet of paper, draw a **sketch** of your design.

Name _____ Date _____

What Happened?

 Read the journal entry.

 Write past tense verbs to complete the entry. Use the Rule Box for help.

Spelling Rules for -ed

- For many verbs, just add **-ed**.

  ask ⟶ ask**ed**

- If the verb ends in a short vowel plus a consonant, double the consonant and add **-ed**.

  stop ⟶ sto(pp)**ed**

- If the verb ends in a consonant plus silent **e**, drop the **e** and add the ending.

  sav~~e~~ ⟶ sav**ed**

- If the verb ends in a consonant plus **y**, change the **y** to **i** and add the ending.

  den~~y~~ ⟶ den**ied**

Dear Journal,

Last week, I ___**entered**___ a writing contest. I _____
          enter   check

my story for any mistakes. I _____ it neatly on paper. Then I
                                      copy

_____ to hear about the results. I _____ the
      wait   ask

mailman if he had a letter for me. I even _____ to find news
                                    try

about the contest on the radio.

This morning, the mailman _____ a letter. I was so
                               deliver

excited, I _____ up and down! My sister _____
        hop   rip

open the envelope. She smiled and said, "I think they _____
                                   like

your story." I won! I was so happy, I almost _____. Then I
                              cry

_____ the letter. It's hanging on my wall.
  frame

For use with TE p. T321

Graphic Organizer: Flow Chart

A Quarter's Worth of Fame

📖 **Review "A Quarter's Worth of Fame."**   ✏️ **Complete the flow chart.**

1. Xander's teacher gives an assignment to design a state quarter.

↓

2. Xander decides to draw the Boston Red Sox. Then he draws a minuteman soldier.

↓

3.

↓

4.

↓

5.

↓

6.

↓

7.

Identify Fact and Opinion

Read the passage below. Think about how to tell a fact from an opinion.

Keep the Air Clean

1   I think air pollution is the biggest problem on earth. Scientists report that air pollution is caused by many things. Some of those things are natural and some are not. Dust and pollen from plants are natural. Smoke from cars and trash that gets into rivers are not. Air pollution can even happen indoors.

2   Scientists have shown that air pollution is bad for people's health. People need air to breathe. Like food and water, air helps us live.

3   As more and more people drive cars, air pollution becomes a bigger problem. I believe that we should not drive cars at all. I think we should take buses. We should also walk or ride bikes more often.

4   In 1970, Americans made a law called The Clean Air Act. The law lets the government make rules to help keep the air clean. Each state has to make sure that everyone follows the rules. For example, cars may not send out as much smoke as they did before 1970. Smoke mixes with fog and becomes smog. The smog stays in the air.

5   Some people think that The Clean Air Act helped stop air pollution. I do not agree. We should do a lot more to solve the problem. We must find new ways to clean the air.

Now take the test on page 89.

Name _____ Date _____

 Test Strategy
Check your answers if you have
time. Reread the questions and
the answers you marked.

Read each item. Choose the best answer.

1   Which sentence is an opinion?

◯   People need air to breathe.

◯   I believe that we should not drive cars at all.

◯   Scientists report that pollution is caused by many things.

◯   Some things that cause pollution are natural, and some are not.

2   Which sentence is a fact?

◯   We should also walk or ride bikes more often.

◯   I believe that we should not drive cars at all.

◯   In 1970, Americans made a law called The Clean Air Act.

◯   We should do a lot more to solve the problem.

3   Complete this sentence with an opinion. Air pollution—

◯   can even happen indoors.

◯   can be bad for people's health.

◯   is caused by many things.

◯   is the biggest problem on earth.

4   Complete this sentence with a fact. Air pollution—

◯   is a terrible thing!

◯   should be stopped.

◯   can happen when smoke mixes with fog.

◯   is the worst problem of our time.

Vocabulary Skill

Confirm Word Meaning

 Study the part of a dictionary page.

✏️ **Write the answer to each question.**

---

state ● stem

state[1] 1. The condition of a person or thing. 2. A smaller unit or part of a country. **state (stāt)** *noun.*

Utah is a state of the U.S.

state[2] To tell in speech or writing. **state (stāt)** *verb.*

statue The shape of a person or animal made of stone, metal, or wood. **statue (stach-yū)** *noun.*

The Statue of Liberty is in New York

stay To remain, stop. **stay (stā)** *verb.*

steal To take something that does not belong to you. **steal (stēl)** *verb.*

---

1. What part of speech is **steal**? _"Steal" is a verb._ _____

2. Could the word **stop** appear on this page? Explain your answer.

   _____

3. Your teacher says, "Texas is a **state**." He also says, "Please **state** the capital of Texas." In which sentence does he use the word **state** as a noun?

   _____

4. Your brother asks you what the word **stay** means. What do you tell him?

   _____

5. Does the word **steal** rhyme with **will** or with **wheel**? _____

   _____

Vocabulary: Key Words

State Words

 Work with a partner.

Read each sentence.

Write *T* for true. Write *F* for false.

Key Words
boundary
capital
government
peace
settlement
treaty

_____ **1.** A **treaty** is a kind of agreement.

_____ **2.** A **settlement** is a person who works in a city.

_____ **3.** There is no war or fighting when there is **peace**.

_____ **4.** The **government** of a state cannot make laws for the state.

_____ **5.** The name of a state **capital** is always the same as the name of the state.

_____ **6.** A **boundary** is where one place stops and another place starts.

MORE Key Words Practice

Find information about your state. Use an encyclopedia or the Internet.

Write three sentences that give information about your state. Be sure to tell about your state's capital and boundaries.

Grammar: Irregular Past Tense Verbs

Fifteen-Questions Game

give?
gave

have?
had

sit?
sat

take?
took

choose?
chose

make?
made

see?
saw

BEGIN

sing?
sang

go?
went

say?
said

keep?
kept

know?
knew

leave?
left

hold?
held

speak?
spoke

THE END

How to Play **Fifteen Questions**

1. Play with a partner. **ẊẊ**

2. Use an eraser or small object as a game piece. Flip a coin to move.
   Heads = 1 space   Tails = 2 spaces

3. Read the words. Use the verb with a question mark to ask a question about "The Tree That Would Not Die." Have your partner use the other verb to answer. For example:
   Question: *Where did the First People choose to meet?*
   Answer: *They chose to meet by an oak tree.*

4. Take turns asking and answering questions.

5. The first one to reach **THE END** wins.

Name _____   Date _____

Persuade

You want your classmates to buy a certain new bike.

 Prepare a short speech to convince your classmates to buy the bike. Use the bandwagon technique.

1. _____

_____

_____

_____

_____

 Now prepare another short speech to convince your classmates to buy the bike. This time, use the repetition technique.

2. _____

_____

_____

_____

_____

MORE Persuasive Techniques

 Get together with two or three classmates.

Present your speeches. Whose speech makes you want to buy the bike most? Talk about the reasons.

Grammar: Irregular Past Tense Verbs

A Tree Grew in Austin

 Read the directions on page 95.

Follow them to make a filmstrip.

Read the directions on page 95.

Past Tense Verbs

| was | fell | built |
| sat | grew | came |

1.

An acorn ___fell___ to the ground.

2.

It _____ into a tree.

3.

A buffalo calf _____ the tree's friend.

4.

The First People _____ under the tree.

5.

The city of Austin _____ a park around the tree.

6.

People _____ to help save the tree.

Grammar: Irregular Past Tense Verbs

A Tree Grew in Austin

Work with a partner.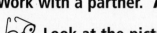

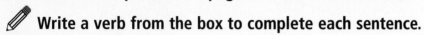 Look at the pictures on page 94. Read the sentences.

Write a verb from the box to complete each sentence.

Color the pictures.

Cut out the pictures.

Put them in order to make a filmstrip.

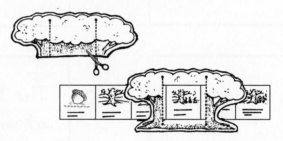

Then cut out the tree.

Cut the lines to the dots to make two slits.

Put your filmstrip through the slits.

Tell the story of the tree to a partner.

MORE Past Tense Verbs

Write about a tree in your neighborhood. Think about the changes your tree has seen over the years. Use past tense verbs to tell the story of the tree.

_____

_____

_____

_____

_____

© Hampton-Brown

Name _____ Date _____

The Tree That Would Not Die

📖 Review "The Tree That Would Not Die."

✏️ Complete the cause-and-effect chart.
Continue on page 97.

Causes	Effects

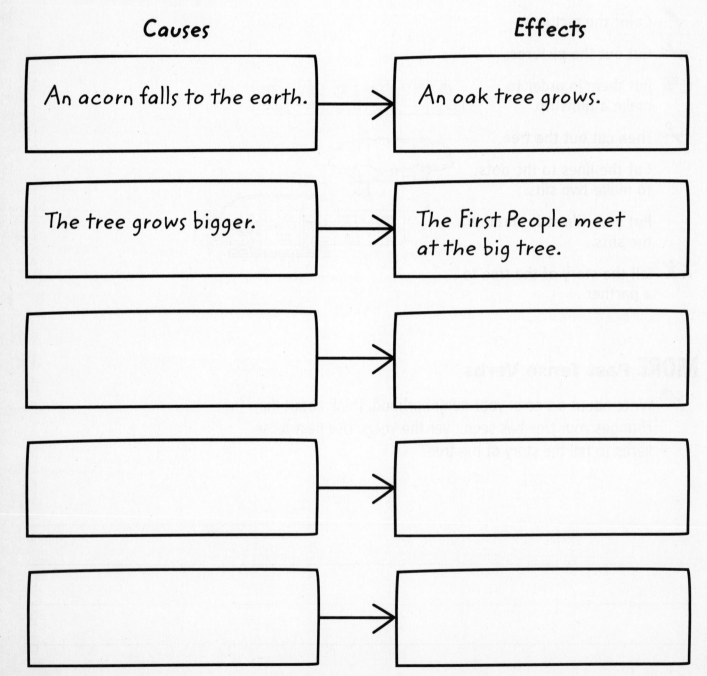

An acorn falls to the earth. → An oak tree grows.

The tree grows bigger. → The First People meet at the big tree.

Graphic Organizer: Cause-and-Effect Chart

The Tree That Would Not Die

Continue the cause-and-effect chart that you started on page 96.

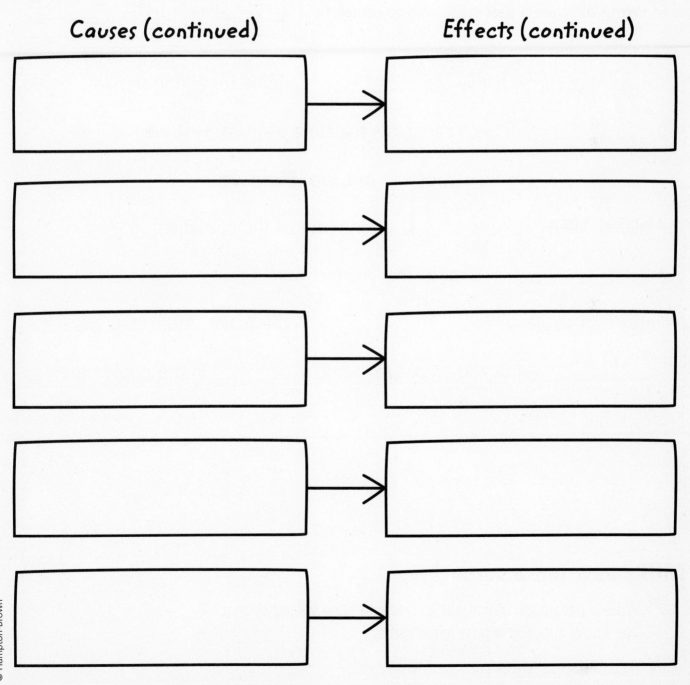

Causes (continued)   Effects (continued)

Name _____ Date _____

I Saw a Great State!

 Read the paragraph.

Change the verb below each blank to tell about the past.

 Write the correct past tense verb to complete the sentence.

Last August, my family _____*left*_____ home for a long trip.
                              leave

We _____ in a car across the state of Texas. First we
       ride

_____ in the city of San Antonio. There we _____
    stop   see

the Alamo. We _____ a long tour of the battlefield.
                   take

We _____ so much that my feet hurt! I _____
       hike   buy

a statue of a soldier who _____ in the battle. After that, we
                                  is

_____ hot and tired. We _____ in the pool at the
    are   swim

motel. It felt great!

MORE Past Tense Verbs

 Write a paragraph. Tell about a state you have visited or that
you know about. Use past tense verbs.

✗✗ Have a partner check your past tense verbs.

Name _____ Date _____

The Oak Will Live!

 Look at the picture. Read the sentence.

Write a future tense verb from the box to complete the sentence.

Future Tense Verbs

am going to watch	will make sure
is going to make	will water
am going to plant	will grow

1. I ___am going to plant___ an acorn.

2. It _____ into a tree.

3. I _____ the tree as it grows.

4. We _____ that no one hurts the tree.

5. People _____ the tree when it is hot.

6. Our tree _____ many other acorns.

© Hampton-Brown

Vocabulary: Key Words

Words at the Market

 Look at the picture. Read the paragraph.

🖊 Then rewrite the paragraph on another sheet of paper. Replace each underlined definition with the correct Key Word.

Key Words
coin
determined
disappointed
goods
load
market
reward

What a Fun Day!

Every Saturday I go to the place where things are sold. I save every metal piece of money I get, so that I can buy many wonderful things. Farmers bring their things to buy, sell, or trade to the market. One farmer carries a large amount of tomatoes in his wagon. He is always trying very hard to sell them all. I never feel like something did not happen the way I wanted at the market on Saturdays. I always have so much fun there! It feels like a gift for doing something good.

For use with TE pp. T378–T379

Name _____ Date _____

Grammar: Present Progressive Verbs

What Are They Doing?

  Look at each picture.

 Complete each sentence with *am*, *is*, or *are* to tell what the people are doing.

Helping Verbs
Use the correct helping verb.

I	**am**
he, she, it	**is**
we, you, they	**are**

1.  They _____*are*_____ riding bicycles.

2.  I _____ counting my money.

3.  The children _____ planting flowers.

4. She _____ carrying a basket.

5.  We _____ walking on the road.

Grammar: Adjectives That Compare

The *Best* Adjectives!

 Read each sentence.

 **Write the correct adjective in each blank.**

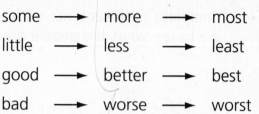

Irregular Adjectives

Some **adjectives** have special forms for comparing things.

some ⟶ more ⟶ most

little ⟶ less ⟶ least

good ⟶ better ⟶ best

bad ⟶ worse ⟶ worst

1. At the market today, I got the _____ vegetables of all.
   more / most

2. The carrots were _____ than the potatoes.
   better / best

3. The green beans were the _____ vegetables.
   best / bestest

4. You bought _____ food than I did.
   less / least

5. Susie has the _____ corn of anyone.
   leaster / least

6. My brother bought _____ fruit than vegetables.
   more / morer

7. Donna got some apples that were _____ than my brother's.
   worse / badder

8. Tom got the _____ apples of all. At least they were cheap!
   worst / worstest

Grammar: Present Perfect Tense

They Have Walked to Market

📖 Look at the page in "My Rows and Piles of Coins."

✏️ Write the present perfect form of the verb to complete each sentence.

Use *has* or *have* and add *-ed*.

> **Which Helping Verb?**
> - Use **has** with **he**, **she**, or **it**.
> - Use **have** with **I**, **you**, **we**, or **they**.

📖 **page 382** 1. Saruni ___has waited___ to buy something.
                        wait

📖 **page 384** 2. He ___has wanted___ a bicycle from the market.
                      want

📖 **page 385** 3. He ___has saved___ coins in a secret money box.
                     save

📖 **page 385** 4. Saruni ___has counted___ his coins.
                        count

📖 **page 386** 5. The children ___have watched___ Saruni every day.
                             watch

📖 **page 386** 6. They ___have laugh___ at him many times.
                      laugh

📖 **page 388** 7. Every week, Yeyo and Saruni ___have walked___ to market.
                                        walk

📖 **page 390** 8. It ___has rain___ for many months.
                     rain

📖 **page 391** 9. Saruni ___has practice___ on his father's bicycle.
                        practice

I have spoken spanish for my whole life.
I have lived in use for 7 months

MORE **Present Perfect Tense**

✏️ Write two sentences about something you have done for a long time. Use a present perfect tense verb in each sentence.

 Share your work with a partner.

Name _____ Date _____

The Market Has Closed

 Read Saruni's journal entry.

✏️ **Write the present perfect form of the verb to complete each sentence.**

Use *has* or *have* and add *-ed*.

> **Which Helping Verb?**
>
> When you form the present perfect tense, be sure the helping verb goes with the subject.
>
> • Use **has** with **he**, **she**, or **it**.
>
> • Use **have** with **I**, **you**, **we**, or **they**.

Dear Journal,

I like to help my mother. I ___*have helped*___ her bring goods to
                              help

market. We _____ there many times. My mom
              walk

_____ me with coins as a reward.
  surprise

The traders _____ their goods on their big tables.
                arrange

I _____ at everything. I _____ with the toys.
  look   play

I _____ one trader about his bicycles. He
  ask

_____ at me many times. My mom _____ to
  laugh   talk

me about it. She has made me feel better.

The farmers _____ their goods into wagons. The traders
                pile

_____ all their goods into boxes. At last the market
  pack

_____.
  close

Graphic Organizer: Goal-and-Outcome Map

My Rows and Piles of Coins

📖 Review "My Rows and Piles of Coins."

✏️ Complete the story map.

Outcome

Event 4

Event 3

Event 2

Event 1

Saruni saves his money. He learns how to ride a bike.

Saruni wants to buy a bicycle.

Goal

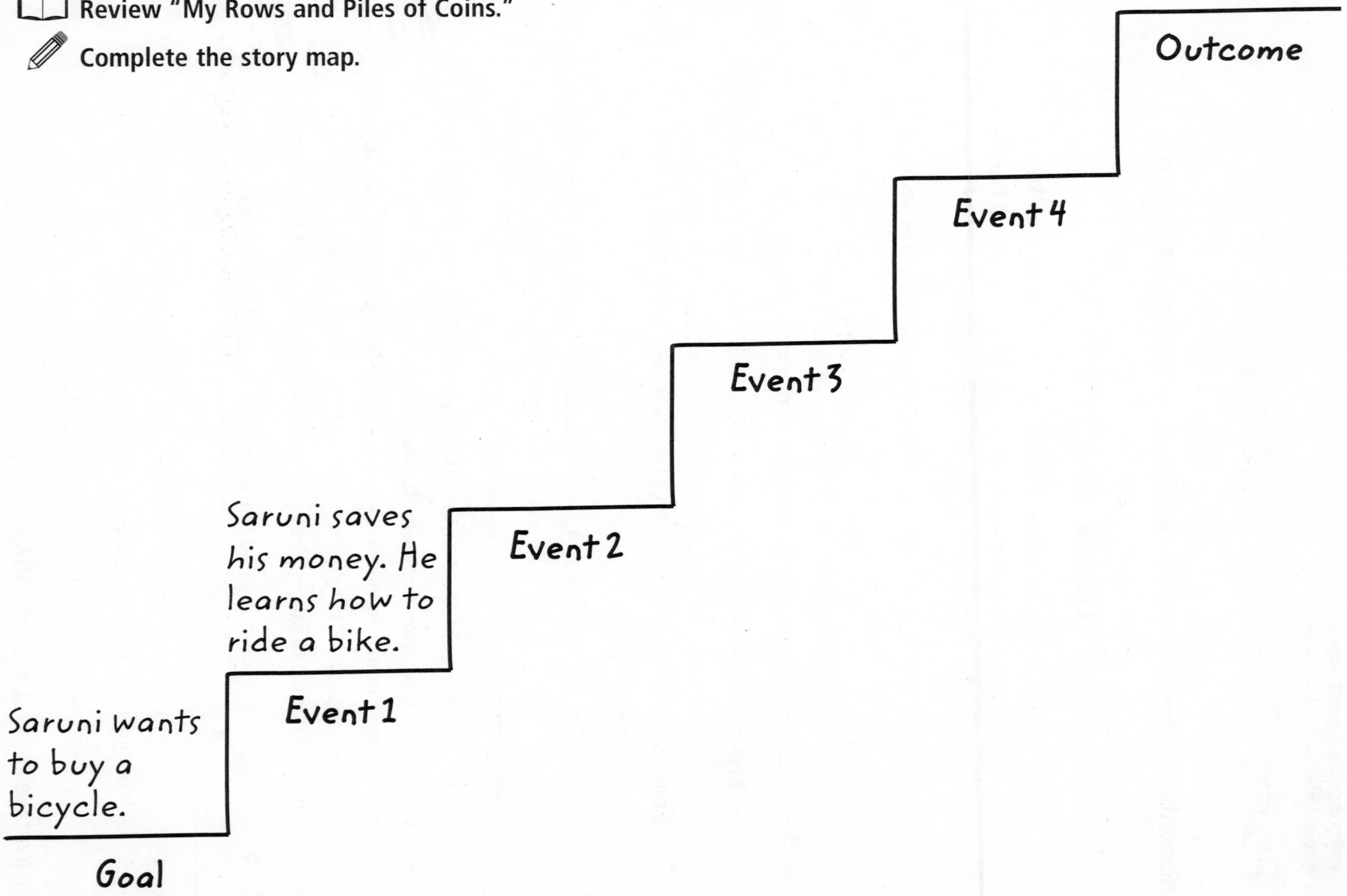

Name _____ Date _____

Form Generalizations

Read the passage below. Think about how to form generalizations.

A Family Money Plan

1   My family wants to buy a video camera for our trip to Africa. My mother is working in Kenya for one month. The whole family will go, too! Her company will pay for almost everything.

2   My father said we can buy the camera if we save enough money. We sat down together to share our plans.

3   My sister Linda plans to baby-sit one night each week and mow lawns. Our neighbors pay a lot of money for that!

4   My brother Paul has a plan, too. He will bring his lunch to school every day. He won't buy lunch in the cafeteria anymore. That will save money. He even plans to make sandwiches for all of us every morning.

5   Keesha, my other sister, will look in the paper for sales on cameras. She thinks that could save us about eighty dollars. Keesha knows how to buy things on sale.

6   My mother said she would talk to friends. She will ask them about the best video camera to buy. Mom says that the most expensive camera is not always the best. Many people pay for extra things that they don't even need. Some people want a camera that looks fancy. They pay more for the style and the color.

7   We all agreed not to spend more money for those things. We just need a simple camera.

8   We will all save money together. My family usually has good ideas. Now our ideas will help us buy a camera.

Now take the test on page 107.

Name _____ Date _____

Test Strategy

Look for important words like *not, which,* and *best* in the questions. They will help you find the correct answer.

Read each item. Choose the best answer.

1   Which generalization best fits the article?

   ⬭   Some plans can help you save money.

   ⬭   Some people want to visit Africa.

   ⬭   Some companies send families on trips.

   ⬭   Some video cameras come with extra things.

2   Which is the best generalization for paragraph 4?

   ⬭   Many schools have cafeterias.

   ⬭   Some students make their own lunches.

   ⬭   Every family needs to eat lunch.

   ⬭   Lunch from home costs less money than lunch from the cafeteria.

3   Which of the following sentences is a generalization?

   ⬭   This camera is on sale.

   ⬭   We will all save money together.

   ⬭   Paul made me a tuna sandwich today.

   ⬭   Many people pay for extra things that they don't even need.

4   Which of the following sentences is *not* a generalization?

   ⬭   Babysitting pays well.

   ⬭   There are many ways to save money.

   ⬭   My mother is working in Kenya for one month.

   ⬭   Many people pay for things they don't need.

Name _____ Date _____

Suffixes

 Read the paragraph.

Fill in the chart. Write the root word, the suffix, and the meaning of each word in dark print.

What Do They Mean?

Suffix	Meaning	Example
-er	a person who	worker
-en	to make; made of	lighten
-ly	in a ____ way	slowly
-y	having	rainy

My father is a **farmer**. He grows many kinds of vegetables. The whole family piles vegetables into **wooden** boxes. We load the boxes into the truck on market day. My father drives **slowly** into town. We want our food to get to market **safely**. We always cover the boxes when it is **stormy**. At the market, I look for the **trader** who sells pens and pencils. I ask her to **sharpen** a pencil for me. I write a list of things to buy. My sister loves **shiny** earrings. I will buy a pair for her birthday.

Root Word	Suffix	Meaning
1. farm	-er	a person who farms
2.		
3.		
4.		
5.		
6.		
7.		
8.		

For use with TE pp. T405a–T405b

Name _____ Date _____

A Fair Trade

Key Words
barter
exchange
service
trade
value

Think about how you might make money or trade things you have to get things you want.

 Complete each sentence.

Share your sentences with a partner.

1. A **service** I could provide to make money would be _____

_____

2. I think this service would have a high **value** because _____

_____

3. I would gladly **trade** or **exchange** my service for money because _____

_____

4. To get something I want without using money, I could **barter** my _____

_____

5. I would **barter** it for _____

_____

MORE Key Words Practice

Choose a partner. Pretend to trade something, like a book for a pen.

Talk about the value of each thing you trade.

Grammar: Simple Subject

Beautiful Items for Sale

 Read each sentence.

 Underline the complete subject. Circle the most important word in the subject.

> **Complete and Simple Subject**
>
> A sentence expresses a complete thought. It has a subject and a predicate. The **subject** tells who or what the sentence is about. The **simple subject** is the most important word in the subject.

1. My older (sister) saves money from her job.

2. Our mother gave her money for something special.

3. My brother drove her to the store.

4. The new jewelry store had many beautiful items.

5. A pretty silver ring was her favorite.

6. A huge crowd waited in line.

7. Smiling customers bought items for sale.

8. She was very happy with her new ring!

MORE Simple Subjects

 Write two sentences about something you bought on sale.

 Read your sentences to a partner.

Have your partner name the simple subject.

Grammar: Simple Predicate

They Love Their Jobs!

 Read each sentence.

✏️ **Underline** the complete predicate. **Circle** the most important word in the predicate.

> **Complete and Simple Predicate**
>
> A sentence expresses a complete thought. It has a subject and a predicate. The **predicate** tells who or what the subject is or does. The **simple predicate** is the verb.

1. My older brother (works) in a bakery.

2. Many people eat his tasty cookies!

3. The butcher loves my brother's bread.

4. Sometimes the two men trade meat for bread.

5. My older sister sells shoes at a store.

6. Some customers buy a lot of shoes.

7. Two girls shop at the store every day!

8. My sister likes her job a lot!

MORE Simple Predicates

👥 Work in a group of three.

💬 Make sentences together. One person chooses a subject. The next person adds a verb, or simple predicate. The third person completes the predicate.

Grammar: Negative Sentences

No, No, No!

 Read each sentence.

 Replace each underlined word to make a negative sentence. Write the new sentence.

1. It is <u>sometimes</u> fun to spend money.

   It is never fun to spend money.

2. <u>Everyone</u> likes to save money.

   _____

3. Banks are <u>always</u> open on the holidays.

   _____

4. <u>Everybody</u> tries to buy items on sale.

   _____

5. Stores have <u>some</u> good sales this time of year.

   _____

 Read each negative sentence.

 Rewrite the sentence using a contraction. Use a separate sheet of paper.

6. People do not use objects as money anymore.

7. Paper money is not too heavy.

8. Most coins in the United States are not made of gold or silver.

> **Ways to Say No**
> • Use these words to make **negative sentences**:
>
>   no   not   no one
>
>   never   nobody
>
> • You can form these **contractions** with **not**:
>
>   is   + not = isn't
>
>   are + not = aren't
>
>   do   + not = don't
>
>   does + not = doesn't

Vocabulary Skill

Context Clues

 Read each group of sentences. Look for clues that tell you what the word in dark print means.

Circle the letter of the correct meaning. Then underline context clues that helped you to choose.

How can kids make money? There is not just one **technique**. There are many ways!

1. What does the word **technique** mean?
   A. way
   B. money
   C. machine

I like to sell lemonade. This service can **generate** a lot of money. I make enough money to pay for movies and snacks.

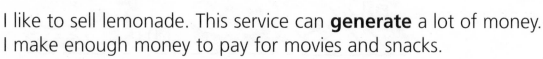

2. What does the word **generate** mean?
   A. find or discover
   B. sell
   C. make or produce

My friend uses shiny rocks to make **ornaments**. People buy these beautiful objects to hang on their walls.

3. What does the word **ornament** mean?
   A. shiny rock
   B. beautiful object
   C. empty wall

Name _____ Date _____

We Work and Play

  Read the paragraph. Look for sentences that have the same subject.

Rewrite the paragraph. Combine the sentences with the same subject to form longer sentences.

> **1 + 1 = 1!**
>
> If two sentences have the same subject, you can combine them to form a longer sentence with a compound predicate.
>
> The family works. The family plays.
>
> The family works **and** plays.

Our family owns a restaurant. My dad cooks. My dad cleans. My uncle likes to talk to customers. They laugh. They eat. I play with my sister. We dance. We sing. My brother is an artist. Frank paints. Frank draws. A special painting hangs on the wall. Everyone loves the painting! The customers look. The customers smile.

_____

_____

_____

_____

_____

_____

_____

Name _____ Date _____

You and I Trade Food

 Study the rules for *and* and *or*. Read the paragraph.

Choose the correct verb to complete each sentence.

Rewrite the paragraph on a separate sheet of paper.

Compound Subject

A **compound subject** is made up of two simple subjects that share the same verb.

• When **and** joins the two subjects, use a verb that tells about more than one.

A penny **and** a nickel <u>are</u> in my pocket.

• When **or** joins the two subjects, use a verb that agrees with the simple subject closest to it.

A penny **or** a nickel <u>is</u> in my pocket.

A quarter **or** two nickels <u>are</u> in this pocket.

My friend and I go to the store. Mary or her parents **(works / work)** there on Mondays. You and I **(shops / shop)** for food. A few dimes and a quarter **(is / are)** in my pocket. The food looks good! The apples and the tomatoes **(shines / shine)**. Two small tomatoes or one large apple **(makes / make)** a nice lunch. I buy some apples, but you buy some tomatoes. You and I **(trades / trade)**. Now we both have apples and tomatoes.

Graphic Organizer: Problem-and-Solution Chain

Money

📖 Review "Money."

✏️ Complete the problem-and-solution chain.

Problems

| People needed things. |

| People couldn't agree on values or find enough people to trade with. |

| The ridum of exchange could be dameged. |

| Metal money wasto havey. |

| |

Solutions

| People traded for what they needed. |

| people develop a ridum of xchange like gold, salt, tea, shells. |

| people invented metal money go it would last longer |

| paper = invented paper money because it was lighter. |

| |

Name _____ Date _____

Compare Unit Prices

Calculate Unit Price

- Find the number of units (items, ounces, grams) in the package.
- Find the price of the package.
- Divide the price by the number of units to find the price per unit.

Sam's Tuna	Bob's Tuna
Units: 10 ounces	Units: 20 ounces
Price: $3.00	Price: $4.00
$3.00 divided by 10 ounces	$4.00 divided by 20 ounces
= $0.30 per ounce	= $0.20 per ounce
Bob's Tuna is a better value!	

Find out the best unit price for a box of cereal.

 Fill in the chart. Calculate the price per unit for each box of cereal.

Which is the best value?

Product	Quantity and Price	Calculations	Price Per Unit
Berry Bear Cereal	unit: 10-ounce box price: $2.50		
Berry Fun Cereal	unit: 15-ounce box price: $3.00		
Bunches of Berries Cereal	unit: 30-ounce box price: $5.00		

Name _____ Date _____

We Are Helping!

 Read each sentence.

 Write the correct helping verb in each blank.

> **Subjects and Helping Verbs**
>
> Sometimes the verbs **am/is/are** and **has/have** are used with other verbs as **helping verbs**. Be sure the helping verb agrees with the subject.
>
> | | | |
> |---|---|---|
> | I | **am** | **have** |
> | you, we, they | **are** | **have** |
> | he, she, it | **is** | **has** |

1. Brent _____ *is* _____ helping his friend Nguyen.

is / are

2. They _____ working at a neighbor's house.

is / are

3. Mrs. Martinez _____ hired them.

has / have

4. Nguyen _____ started to paint the house.

has / have

5. Brent _____ cleaning the garage.

is / are

6. Nguyen and Brent _____ opened savings accounts.

has / have

7. They _____ saving money for college.

is / are

8. Mrs. Martinez _____ happy that she hired the boys.

is / are

9. They _____ offered to work all summer.

has / have

Name _David Tecualt_ Date _04/5/06_

Negative Prefixes

 Read the paragraph.

Write a word with a prefix that means the same as the words under the blank.

Prefix Chart		
Prefix	**Meaning**	**Example**
im-	not	impossible
in-	not	incomplete
non-	not, without	nonfiction
mis-	bad or wrong	misbehave

My friend Sue Ann and I had a __*misunderstanding*__ about money.

wrong understanding

Sue Ann thinks it is ___impossible___ to earn money on your own.

not possible

I told her she is ___misinformed___. There are many ways to earn money!

wrongly informed

"Yes," Sue Ann said, "if you work ___nonstop___. Besides, things are

without stop

just too expensive!" I reminded Sue Ann of many ___inexpensive___ items.

not expensive

Sue Ann decided she was being ___impatient___. She said, "It is

not patient

just _____ to think I can't earn money." Sue Ann is going to

not correct

look for a job tomorrow!

MORE Negative Prefixes

✏️ Write one sentence that uses the word *possible*. Write another sentence that uses the word *correct*.

👥 Trade sentences with a partner. Rewrite the sentences using the words *impossible* and *incorrect*.

Name David Tecuott   Date 0614/06

Words at a Museum

✏️ **Write a Key Word to complete each sentence.**

🏃 **Check your work with a partner.**

Key Words
~~abandon~~
~~enormous~~
~~journey~~
~~lift~~
~~lonely~~
meteorite
~~museum~~
~~strain~~

1. Yesterday I felt sad and _____lonely_____ without my best friend.

2. Anna went on a long _____journey_____ to see her family in Norway.

3. My mom took me to the science _____museum_____. She thought it would make me feel better.

4. I told her not to _____abandon_____ me, or I might get lost.

5. We saw an _____enormous_____ rock!

6. It was a rock from outer space, called a _____meteorite_____.

7. My brother pretended to _____lift_____ the rock above his shoulders.

8. My mom said even a full-grown man would have to _____strain_____ to pick up that rock!

MORE Key Words Practice

👓 Look for pictures of meteorites in a science book or encyclopedia.

✏️ Draw a picture of a meteorite.

✏️ Write a sentence that tells about it.

For use with TE pp. T436–T437

Grammar: Compound Sentences

The Meteorite

 Study how to combine sentences. Then read each pair of sentences.

Combine the two sentences. Use _and, but,_ or _or._

> ### Combine Sentences
> When you put two sentences together, use a **comma** before **and, but,** or **or**.
> - Use **and** to join ideas that are alike.
> - Use **but** for ideas that are different.
> - Use **or** for a choice between two ideas.

1. The meteorite saw the people. They did not see it.

The meteorite saw the people, but they did not see it.

2. Finally some people came. They looked at the meteorite.

_____

_____

3. They thought it might be an earth rock. It might be a meteorite.

_____

_____

4. They loaded it into their car. They brought it to a museum.

_____

_____

5. They were glad to bring it to the museum. They were sad when they left.

_____

_____

Vocabulary Skill

Multiple-Meaning Words

👓 Read each sentence. Then read each meaning of the word in dark print.

✏️ Circle the letter of the correct meaning in the sentence. <u>Underline</u> the clues that helped you choose it.

1. I looked up the **address** of the museum to find <u>what street it is on.</u>

(a.) An **address** tells the location of a place.

b. An **address** is a speech that someone gives.

c. When you **address** an envelope, you write where to send it.

2. All the meteorites traveled through outer **space** before they hit Earth.

(a.) **Space** is the area all around Earth.

b. Words in a sentence are separated by a blank **space**.

c. You can park your car in a parking **space**.

3. A strange meteorite landed in the **state** of Wisconsin.

a. When you **state** something, you say it in words.

(b.) A **state** is a part of the United States, like Iowa or New York.

c. Your **state** of mind is how you feel.

4. It was not a heavy meteorite. It was **light** and easy to pick up.

a. The bright **light** from a lamp can help you see.

b. A **light** color is not dark.

(c.) Something is **light** if it is not heavy.

Name _____ Date _____

Character's Point of View

Think of a story you have read, or a movie you have seen. Think of a character that was NOT the main character. How do you think that character thought or felt?

 Write the title of the story or movie and the name of the character. Then tell the story from that character's point of view.

Story or Movie: _____

Character: _____

What the Character Thinks:

_____

_____

_____

_____

_____

_____

_____

_____

_____

_____

Graphic Organizer: Character Chart

Call Me Ahnighito

📖 Review "Call Me Ahnighito."   ✏️ Complete the character chart.

	How Ahnighito feels	Why Ahnighito feels that way
pages 440-442	lonely, bored	Ahnighito sits in the Arctic all day. Nothing happens there.
	worried, scared	People begin to chip away at him.
	joyful, free	People roll Ahnighito into the sun.
pages 443-445	Happy	the new people had come Backo.
	exited	The people were thing to lift the roak.
pages 446-449	Happy	the people was taking the rock away.
	excited	Because he was goin to meas a new place.
	happy	because he was in a Knew place.
pages 450-452	confused	Because he Dir't know over the people was goin to take him.
	scard	Because people were tralling to tuch him.
	happy	Because every one knoo his name and oloolen of him

Name David Tacuett   Date 04/11/06

Read a Road Map

Highways in the Austin Area

Study the map.

Write the answer to each question.

KEY
- ⬡ Highway Route
- ★ State Capital
- ■ City

Miles
0 25 50 75 100

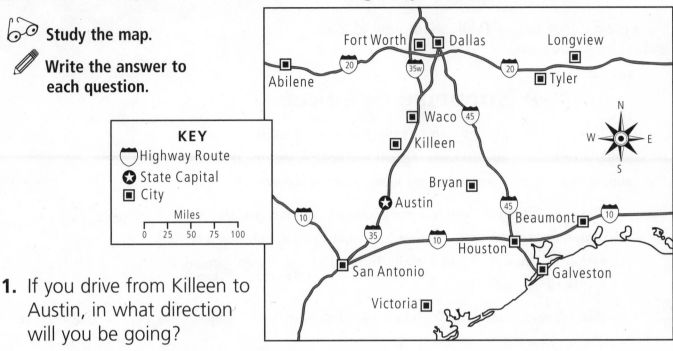

1. If you drive from Killeen to Austin, in what direction will you be going?

   I Will be goin South.

2. Which highway route would you use to drive from Dallas to Houston?

   I would yoas hightway 45.

3. If you drive from Waco to Dallas, in what direction will you be going?

   I would by goin to North

4. About how many miles are between San Antonio and Houston?

   Like 145 mile.

5. Which highway would you take to go from Abilene to Longview?

   I will take Hightway Rute 45.

6. What is the name of the state capital shown on this map?

   the state capital

© Hampton-Brown

Comprehension Skill

Make and Revise Predictions

Read the passage below. Think about how to make and revise predictions.

A Surprise Speaker

1   This morning, Ms. Ignacio, our teacher, said, "I have a treat for you! After lunch you will hear a great lecture." A lecture is a talk someone gives to share facts and ideas about a subject.

2   She said, "Our lecturer is a rock collector named Ali Ahmad. He is an expert, because he knows a lot about rocks. I saw him on television last month. Then I wrote him a letter. I asked him to come talk to us. Today he is here!"

3   "Ms. Ignacio," asked my friend Chris, "How long does it take to become an expert?"

4   "It takes a long time," said our teacher. "Some people say it takes a lifetime. Ali Ahmad has collected rocks for many years. He has learned all about them. Some of his rocks are in museums around the world!"

5   We walked to the lecture hall after lunch. Two people waited on the stage. There was a man with gray hair and a teenage boy.

6   "The man with the gray hair must be Mr. Ahmad," said Chris.

7   "Yes," I agreed. "So the boy must be his grandson. Why do you think he came, too?"

8   "I guess he wants to learn a little bit about rocks, too," said Chris.

Now take the test on page 127.

Name _David Tecco??_ Date _04/11/06_

Test Strategy
Read all of the answer choices
before you choose an answer.

Read each item. Choose the best answer.

1   Read the story again. What prediction can you make about the lecture?

   ⊂▬⊃ The students will speak.

   ⊂▬⊃ The teenage boy will speak.

   ⊂▬⊃ The teacher, Ms. Ignacio, will speak.

   ⊂▬⊃ The man with gray hair will speak.

2   Read the passage.

> We were all surprised when the teenage boy
> started to talk. He was Ali Ahmad! He knows all
> about rocks. He began to learn about them when he
> was only five years old. The man with the gray hair
> was the director of a museum. He came because he
> wanted to meet Ali.

Revise your prediction.

   ⊂▬⊃ No one gave the lecture.

   ⊂▬⊃ The teacher gave the lecture.

   ⊂▬⊃ The teenage boy gave the lecture.

   ⊂▬⊃ The man with gray hair gave the lecture.

3   Which of the following is *not* a good prediction about Ali?

   ⊂▬⊃ Ali will continue to study rocks.

   ⊂▬⊃ Ali will help others learn about rocks.

   ⊂▬⊃ Ali will enjoy talking to students about rocks.

   ⊂▬⊃ Ali will stop studying rocks tomorrow.

Name David Teccott   Date 09/11/00

Interpret Maps

Meteorite Craters in Australia

 Study the map.

Write the answer to each question.

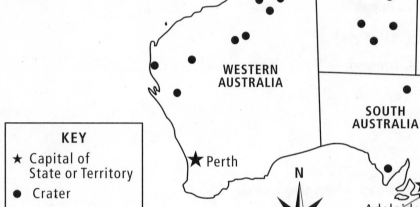

KEY
★ Capital of State or Territory
● Crater

Darwin ★

NORTHERN TERRITORY

WESTERN AUSTRALIA

QUEENSLAND

SOUTH AUSTRALIA

Brisbane ★

NEW SOUTH WALES

★ Perth

Adelaide

VICTORIA

Sydney

Melbourne

N W E S

1. What does the map show?

The map shows meteorite craters in Australia.

2. What is the capital city of Queensland?

Brisbane

3. Which two states shown have no craters?

Victoria, New south Wales ✓

4. Are there more craters in northern or southern Australia?

Northern

5. Is Sydney located on the east coast or west coast of Australia?

West coast of Australia.

Name _David Tecua H_____ Date _05/22/06_____

Charts and Diagrams

👓 Study the diagram and the chart.

✏️ Write the answer to each question.

Meteorite Craters Around the World

Name	Location	Diameter (in kilometers)
Barringer	United States	1.2
Liverpool	Australia	1.6
Lonar	India	1.8
Viewfield	Canada	2.5

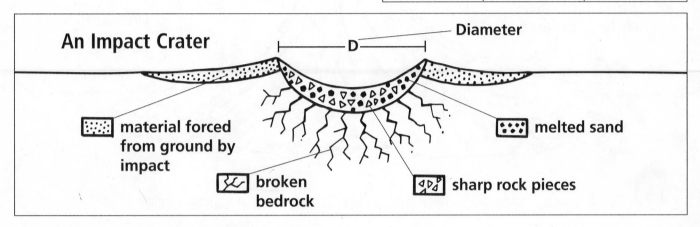

An Impact Crater — Diameter

▦ material forced from ground by impact

▧ broken bedrock

▨ sharp rock pieces

▦ melted sand

1. What does the diameter show?

The diameter Shows the sice of the meteorite.

2. What happens to bedrock when a meteorite hits Earth?

When a meteorite hit the Earth make a hole.

3. Where is the Lonar Crater located?

India.

4. What is the diameter of the Barringer Crater?

United states.

5. What material can you find at the bottom of an impact crater?

You can see melte sand, Sharp rock picces and broken bedrock

6. What is the name of the crater with the largest diameter?

Viewfeild Canada 2.5.

Name David Teccialt   Date 05/22/06

Rocky Words

Key Words

| cycle |
| erosion |
| layer |
| liquid |
| magma |
| pressure |
| solid |
| weathering |

👫 **Work with a partner.**

👓 **Read each sentence.**

✏️ **Write *T* for true.**
Write *F* for false.

____T____ **1.** A **cycle** happens over and over again in the same order.

____T____ **2.** One thing pushing against another thing can cause **pressure**.

____F____ **3.** **Weathering** is a way to tell when a storm is coming.

____T____ **4.** If something is **liquid**, it is very hot.

____T____ **5.** **Magma** is found underground.

____F____ **6.** A **layer** is one thickness of something.

____T____ **7.** Air is an example of a **solid** material.

____T____ **8.** **Erosion** can break apart rocks.

MORE Key Words Practice

💬 Make up a sentence with two of the Key Words. Tell it to a partner. 👫

Grammar: Complex Sentences

When Rocks Get Hot, They Melt

👫 **Work with a partner.**

👓 **Read each pair of sentences.**

    Put the two sentences together to make one sentence. Combine them using *when*.

✏️ **Write the sentence.**

1. Magma reaches the surface. A volcano erupts.

When magma reaches the surface, a volcano erupts.

2. Crystals are large. Rock cools slowly.

When Rock cools Slowly, Crystals are large.

3. Tiny particles can break off a rock. Wind blows sand against it.

When Wind blows sand agains it, tiny particles can break off a rock.

4. Particles of rock can travel far away. The wind blows them away.

When The wind blows them away, particles of rock can travel far away.

5. The color of rocks is changed. They go through high heat and pressure.

Name _____ Date _____

Do This Carefully!

 Read each sentence.

 Write an adverb that tells *how*, *where*, or *when*. **Use an adverb from the box or think of a different one.**

Adverbs
You can use an **adverb** to give more details. An adverb can tell how, where, or when.

how	where	when
quickly	there	then
slowly	here	yesterday
carefully	down	always

1. I went to collect rocks _____ *yesterday* _____ .

when

2. I walked _____ to the crater of an old volcano.

how

3. I looked _____ into the bottom of the crater.

where

4. _____ I saw a big lake surrounded by volcanic rock.

where

5. When a volcano erupts, lava flows _____ down its sides.

how

6. It cools _____ into solid rock.

how

7. _____ I went to look at a crystal cave.

when

8. The atoms of each kind of crystal _____ arrange themselves in the same way.

when

MORE Adverbs

Choose one adverb from the box at the top of the page.

Make up one sentence that uses the adverb. Tell it to a partner. **ẊẊ**

Grammar: Complex Sentences

Because They Are Rocks!

Look at the cause-and-effect chart.

Use the word *because* to combine the sentences.
Write the new sentence.

Cause-and-Effect Chart

Effects	Causes
1. Rocks melt.	1. It is hot deep inside the earth.
2. Each kind of crystal always has its own shape.	2. The atoms are arranged in the same way.
3. Tiny pieces break off a rock.	3. Water pounds on the rock.
4. Some people wear diamonds.	4. Diamonds sparkle.
5. People use rocks to make walls.	5. Rocks are strong.

1. Rocks melt because it is hot deep inside the earth.

2. _____

3. _____

4. _____

5. _____

Name David Tecualt   Date 05/25/06

Graphic Organizer: Outline

The Life Story of a Rock

Review "The Life Story of a Rock."

Complete the outline.

I. Rocks are born. (pages 464-466)

A. Earth has layers.

B. Volcanoes form igneous rocks.

II. Rocks change and move. (pages 467-471)

A. Rock change Because of wethering.

B. Rock travels because strong.

C. Rock chage with air, presser and heat.

D. With Time the Rock Chage as wather and sand make it biger.

III. Rocks are useful. (pages 472-475)

A. contruction.

B. A cougar finds shelter in a cave.

C. To make decorations.

D. for Plants to grow.

© Hampton-Brown

134 Unit 8 | Rocky Tales   For use with TE pp. T476–T477

Name ___David Tevalt___   Date __05/26/06__

Say It in One Sentence!

👓 **Read each pair of sentences.**

✏️ **Combine the two sentences. Use the word *but, when, and, or,* or *because*.**

1. This rock is heavy. I cannot lift it.

This rock is heavy, and I cannot lift it.

2. I wanted to take it home. I collect rocks.

I collect rocks, when I wated to tak it Home.

3. My friend thought he found a rose quartz. I did not agree.

My fiend thought he found a rose quartz, but I did not agree.

4. Rocks can wear away quickly. They can wear away slowly.

5. Rocks are exciting. You love them as much as I do.

MORE Sentences

👫 Work with a partner. Write five complex sentences. Each sentence should use *but, when, and, or,* or *because*.

Grammar: Prepositions and Adverbs

Tell Me More!

📖 **Look at the page in "The Life Story of a Rock."**

✏️ Write the correct word or words that tell *where, when,* or *how* to complete each sentence.

👫 **Check your work with a partner.**

> ### Prepositions and Adverbs
>
> Use words that tell **when, where,** and **how** to give more information.
>
> He collects rocks.
>
> <u>Daily</u>, he <u>happily</u> collects rocks <u>in the hills</u>.
>   when   how   where

📖 **page 464** 1. Some rocks are born ___*inside the earth*___.
                                    inside the earth / by a tree

📖 **page 464** 2. Lava can flow _____ down a volcano.
                                      quickly / tightly

📖 **page 466** 3. Some rocks are crystals _____.
                                    from beautiful shapes / with beautiful shapes

📖 **page 467** 4. _____ cold nights, rainwater freezes.
                                  During / Before

📖 **page 468** 5. A rock can travel far _____ where it was born.
                                  from the place / into the place

📖 **page 469** 6. Sediment settles _____ of water.
                                    to the bottom / to the top

📖 **page 471** 7. A rock's life cycle repeats _____.
                                  for many years / for a few days

📖 **page 472** 8. Trees hold _____ to rocks on windy days.
                              loosely / tightly

MORE Prepositions and Adverbs

✏️ Write a paragraph. Tell about something you did last week.

Use words that tell *where, when,* or *how* in your paragraph.

👫 Share your work with a partner.